Collapse Now and Avoid the Rush

Collapse Now and Avoid the Rush

The Best of *The Archdruid Report*

John Michael Greer

FOUNDERS HOUSE
PUBLISHING
2015

Collapse Now and Avoid the Rush: The Best of *The Archdruid Report*
Copyright © 2015 John Michael Greer
Published by Founders House Publishing, LLC
Front cover art © Masta4650/Dreamstime.com
Cover and internal design © 2015 Founders House Publishing, LLC

Paperback Edition: March 2015
ISBN: 978-0692389454

For more information please visit www.foundershousepublishing.com

Published in the United States of America

Contents

Collapse Now and Avoid the Rush

Introduction

In the spring of 2006, I decided to start a blog. It was in some ways an odd decision for me, since I had (and have) no great fondness for computer technology or online culture. Still, there was a point to the exercise, though I suspect many readers will find my reason odder than the decision itself: I wanted to start a conversation about the future of industrial society among members of the contemporary Druid community.

The contemporary Druid community? Most people aren't aware of this, but there is one. According to the one scholarly study of that community, a French doctoral dissertation from 1984, there are something like two million of us worldwide. Modern Druidry is about three centuries old, and its founders back in the eighteenth century were inspired by, rather than descended from, the wizards and scholars of the ancient Celtic peoples who originally wore the title "Druid." It's not so much an organized religion as a disorganized one, being comfortably divided into dozens of loose affiliations whose members rarely find it necessary to agree on much. Eccentric as it is, it's my spiritual home; in the spring of 2006, I had been a Druid for twelve years, and was into my third year as the presiding officer of the Ancient Order of Druids in America (AODA).

The future of industrial society? That's an even more complicated and contentious issue. When I was coming of age in the 1970s, it was fairly common to find people seriously worried about

1

the future of industrial society, and for good reason. Scientists from the whole spectrum of relevant disciplines warned that unless the world's industrial nations changed course dramatically and soon, the world was facing deep trouble sometime in the early to middle decades of the 21st century. That awareness went by the boards in the Reagan years, but the problems themselves didn't go away. By 2006 it was becoming brutally clear that the warnings had been square on target, and the airy insistence that technology and the market would triumph over mere ecological realities was either dishonest or deranged.

It so happens that I studied environmental sciences, organic gardening, and appropriate technology back in the late 1970s and early 1980s, and managed not to lose track of those things during industrial society's thirty-year vacation from reality. In the late 1990s, when the first whispers of trouble with fossil fuel depletion and carbon dioxide buildup in the atmosphere were starting to echo through the crawlspaces of our culture, I went back to my shelf of old ecology books and found their insights and warnings as cogent as ever.

Right about that same time, "peak oil"—a convenient bit of verbal shorthand for "the global peak of conventional petroleum production"—began to find its way into the collective conversation of our time. Thereafter, for the first time in decades, peak oil books such as Richard Heinberg's *The Party's Over* and James Howard Kunstler's *The Long Emergency* found an audience. I drew in a deep breath and decided that it was time to get a conversation about such things going in the Druid community.

That was the genesis of *The Archdruid Report*, which went online on May 6, 2006. I honestly thought that I'd be lucky to get fifteen readers. It wasn't just that I was writing on an unfashionable subject for a limited audience; everything I'd read about blogging insisted that long essays making complex arguments about uncomfortable topics were the kiss of death. The subjects I wanted to explore, though, couldn't be explored in any meaningful way without doing all three of these things, so I started posting—irregularly at first, and then once a week, on Wednesday evenings, as I got into the rhythm of the work.

By the autumn of 2006, I'd gotten my fifteen readers, and was delighted to field two or three comments to each weekly post. That's when things started to get strange. The number of comments started to lurch unsteadily upwards, so did the number of page views, and other blogs started linking back to weekly posts of mine or simply reposting them intact. I noted the shift, and guessed that *The Archdruid Report* was getting its fifteen minutes of very limited fame. No doubt, I thought, things would get back to normal in a few months.

They didn't: not then, and not thereafter. As I write these words, *The Archdruid Report* fields upwards of a quarter million unique page views each month. Each weekly post is reposted on anything up to two hundred other blogs, while hundreds more discuss, expand, critique, and denounce the ideas I've tried to present. Meanwhile explorations from *The Archdruid Report* have provided raw material for ten books of mine, two of them popular novels, and an anthology of deindustrial science fiction. What started as a quiet conversation among Druids has turned into something considerably larger.

Thus I was pleased when Founders House Publishing, which has already published my post-peak oil SF novel *Star's Reach*, asked about the possibility of publishing a collection of posts from *The Archdruid Report* that hadn't found their way into my books. It so happens that many of the most popular posts weren't suitable raw material for book projects, and some of the ones that were had to be reworked so drastically that very little of the original post remained. It was an easy matter to sort out twenty-five posts that, to my mind, show *The Archdruid Report* at its best; I gave them the bare minimum of editing and footnotes that the changed format required, and the result is the book you're now reading.

Over the last eight and a half years, I've wondered tolerably often why it is that any of this happened. Authors are notoriously the last people to ask about the reasons for the popularity (or lack of same) of their work, but after any number of conversations with readers, I think I can venture a speculation. I've come to think that a significant number of people are tired of the glib chatter that fills so much of popular culture these days; they've recognized that there's not actually that much that can be said in short, snappy tweets illustrated with cute-puppy photos, and forcing discourse within such limits does not exactly help in facing the rising spiral of crises that defines our troubled age. (If a potter makes pots, one might ask, what does Twitter make?) Thus there's a far more substantial audience than I or anyone else seems to have suspected for serious efforts to get past the crackpot optimism of the last three decades, and grapple with the shape of the bleak future we've made for ourselves.

It was the presence of that audience, more than anything else, that took *The Archdruid Report* and turned it into something more than a quiet conversation among Druids. For eight years now, I've had the good fortune to benefit from comments, critiques, challenges, and furious denunciations from many thousands of readers. Those who responded with enthusiasm to the ideas I proposed helped keep me going through the inevitable difficult times, while those who rejected what I had to say, in modes that varied from the thoughtful to the foam-flecked, provided entertainment even when they failed to offer anything more useful. To all of them, to everyone who's read *The Archdruid Report* during its first eight and a half years, this collection is dedicated.

—John Michael Greer
Cumberland, MD 2014

Real Druids

(Originally published 6 May 2006)

This year's Earth Day in Ashland, Oregon, where I live, featured an interfaith service at the local Unitarian church, and I wasn't too surprised to get a call inviting me to be one of the presenters. Like the other interfaith events I've been to, this one was sparsely attended but enthusiastic; a choir sang upbeat songs about saving the planet in between snippets of Buddhist sutras, Baha'i prayers, Taoist poetry, and yes, a bit of Druid ritual. Afterwards, though, as I was folding up my robes, a kid about eight years old came into the little alcove where the presenters stashed their gear, looked up at me and asked, "Are you a *real* Druid?"

Half an hour later, as I walked home through Oregon rain, the question still burned.

It's not an easy question to answer. The original Druids, the priests and wizards of the ancient Celts, went extinct more than a thousand years ago, and all their beliefs, practices, and teachings went with them. Maybe they were the wise oak-priests of today's historical fantasies, maybe they were the "obscure barbarian priesthood of interest only to specialists" that historians like the late Stuart Piggott prefer to imagine. We'll never know, because they and almost everything connected with them vanished in the early Dark Ages.

Some modern Druid groups in the nineteenth and early twentieth centuries, to their lasting discredit, claimed direct connections to the ancient Celtic Druids they didn't have. The real roots of the modern

Druid movement go in a different direction: to the first stages of the Industrial Revolution in early eighteenth century Britain, and the Hobson's choice between dogmatic religion and materialist science, the two victors in the reality wars of the late Renaissance. Plenty of people sought a third option that embraced nature and spirit alike, and some of them found inspiration in the scraps of classical writing, medieval legend, and Celtic folklore that referred to the ancient Druids.

Historians call the result the Druid Revival. By the middle years of the eighteenth century there were organized Druid groups active in Britain, and by the beginning of the next century the Revival spread to America and France. The Druid order I head, the Ancient Order of Druids in America (AODA), was founded in 1912, so to some extent we're the new kid on the block: part of a tradition that's been active in the western world for close to three centuries, proclaiming in its quiet way the holiness of nature and the need for human beings to return to harmony with the living Earth.

That's a message that could bear repeating these days. I don't think it's an accident that the Druid Revival started alongside the Industrial Revolution, as the western world began to launch itself on a trajectory that's bringing it up against hard planetary limits in our own time. Those first modern Druids pointed out the road our civilization didn't take, a sustainable path in harmony with the living world. The ancient Celtic Druids whose example inspired them lived in a different age, with different challenges, but their reverence for forests and the powers of nature still guides and motivates Druids today.

I can't say that all this went through my mind as I fumbled for an answer to the kid's question, but when you use the word "Druid" for yourself and your spirituality nowadays, issues like these are never far away. "Yes," I told him finally. "Yes, I am."

He grinned, and said, "I thought so. Thanks!" Then he scampered off, and I walked home through the rain with history spinning in my head.

Knowing Only One Story

(Originally published 24 May 2006)

The Druid way can be followed anywhere, but for me, at least, it's always a bit easier outside among green growing things. That doesn't require wilderness; some of the most transformative experiences of my own Druid path took place in a week of dawn meditations in the gardens in Chalice Well in Glastonbury, which hasn't been wilderness any time in the last five thousand years. Still, there's much to be said for a creekside meadow up in the Oregon Cascades, with the sun just beginning to burn through morning mist and the distant noises of the breakfast crew back at camp drowned out by birdsong and running water. That's where I was, in the middle of my dawn meditation, when three sentences whispered themselves in the silence inside my head.

Knowing many stories is wisdom.
Knowing no stories is ignorance.
Knowing only one story is death.

I've been brooding about those sentences for the year and a half since that morning, and the more I think about them the more they say to me about where we are today and how we got here.

Traditional cultures around the world have a wealth of stories, and a very large part of education in those cultures consists of sharing, learning, and thinking about those stories. They aren't simply entertainment. Stories are probably the oldest and most important of all human tools. We think with stories, by fitting the "blooming, buzzing confusion" of the universe around us into narrative patterns that make the world make sense. Even today, we use stories to tell us who we are, what the world is like, and what we can and can't do with our lives. It's just that nowadays the stories have changed.

One of the most striking things about old stories, the stories of traditional cultures, is that no two of them have the same moral. Think of the fairy tales you grew up with. They put different people in different situations with very different results. Sometimes violating a prohibition brought success ("Jack and the Beanstalk"), sometimes it brought disaster ("Sleeping Beauty"). Sometimes victory went to the humble and patient ("Cinderella"), sometimes it went to the one who was willing to try the impossible ("Puss in Boots"). There are common themes in the old stories, of course, but endless variations on them. Those differences are a source of great power. If you have a wealth of different stories to think with, odds are that whatever the world throws at you, you'll be able to find a narrative pattern that makes sense of it.

Over the last few centuries, though, the multiple-narrative approach of traditional cultures has given way, especially in the industrial West, to a way of thinking that privileges a single story above all others. Think of any currently popular political or religious ideology, and you'll likely find at its center the claim that one and only one story explains everything in the world.

For fundamentalist Christians, it's the story of Fall and Redemption ending with the Second Coming of Christ. For Marxists, it's the very similar story of dialectical materialism ending with the dictatorship of the proletariat. For rationalists, neoconservatives, most scientists, and quite a fair number of ordinary people in the developed world, it's the story of progress. The political left and right each has its own story, and the list goes on.

One symptom of knowing only one story is the certainty that whatever problem comes up, it has the same solution. For fundamentalist Christians, no matter what the problem, the solution is surrendering your will to Jesus—or, more to the point, to the guy who claims to be able to tell you who Jesus wants you to vote for. For Marxists, the one solution for all problems is proletarian revolution. For neoconservatives, it's the free market. For scientists, it's more scientific research and education. For Democrats, it's electing Democrats; for Republicans, it's electing Republicans.

The problem is that the universe is what ecologists call a complex system. In a complex system, feedback loops and unexpected consequences make a mockery of simplistic attempts to predict effects from causes, and no one solution will effectively respond to more than a small portion of the challenges the system can throw at you. This leads to the second symptom of knowing only one story, which is repeated failure.

Recent economic history offers a good example. For the last two decades, free-market advocates in the World Bank and the International Monetary Fund (IMF) have been pushing a particular set of reforms on governments and economies around the world, insisting that these reforms are the one and only solution to every economic ill. Everywhere those have been fully implemented, the result has been economic and social disaster—think East Asia in the late 1980s, or Russia and Latin America in the 1990s—and the countries devastated by these "reforms" have returned to prosperity only after reversing them. None of this has stopped the free market's true believers from continuing to press forward toward the imaginary Utopia their story promises them.

If you know plenty of stories, and know how to think with them, the complexity of the universe is less of a problem, because you have a much better chance of being able to recognize what story the universe seems to be following, and act accordingly. If you don't know any stories at all, interestingly, you may still get by; even though you don't have the resources of story wisdom to draw on, you may still be able to judge the situation on its own merits and act accordingly; you have flexibility.

But if you only know one story, and you're committed to the idea that the world makes sense if and only if it's interpreted through the filter of that one story, you're stuck in a rigid stance with no options for change. Much more often than not, you fail, since the complexity of the universe is such that no single story makes a useful tool for understanding more than a very small part of it. If you can recognize this and let go of your story, you can begin to learn. If you've gotten your ego wrapped up in the thought of having the one and only true story, though, and you try to force the world to fit your story rather than allowing your story to change to fit the world, the results will not be good.

This leads to the third symptom of knowing only one story, which is rage. Failure is a gift because it offers the opportunity for learning, but if the gift is too emotionally difficult to accept, the easy way out is to take refuge in rage. When we get angry with people who disagree with us about politics or religion, I'm coming to think, what really angers us is the fact that our one story doesn't fit the universe everywhere and always, and those who disagree with us simply remind us of that uncomfortable fact.

Plenty of pundits, and many ordinary people, as well have commented on the extraordinary level of anger that surges through America these days. From talk radio to political debates to everyday conversations, dialogue has given way to diatribe across the political spectrum. It's unlikely to be a coincidence that this has happened over a quarter century when the grand narratives of both major American political parties failed the test of reality. The 1960s and 1970s saw the Democrats get the chance to enact the reforms they wanted; the 1980s and the first decade of the 21st century saw the Republicans get the same opportunity. Both parties found themselves stymied by a universe that obstinately refused to play along with their stories, and too often, people on both sides turned to anger and scapegoating as a way to avoid having to rethink their ideas.

That habit of rage isn't going to help us, or anyone, as we move toward a future that promises to leave most of our culture's familiar stories in tatters. As we face the unwelcome realities of resource depletion, environmental instability, and the inevitable hangover coming on the heels of our fictive economy's decades-long binge, clinging to whatever single story appeals to us may be emotionally comforting in the short term, but it leads down a dead end familiar to those who study the history of extinct civilizations. Learning other stories, and finding out that it's possible to see the world in more than just one way, is a more viable path.

The Twelfth Hour

(Originally published 29 August 2007)

One of the things I've noted repeatedly since *The Archdruid Report* first began attracting a significant number of comments is the way that certain stories maintain a deathgrip on our collective imagination of the future. I've written at length in previous posts here about two of those stories, the story of progress and the story of survivalism. Look through the last decade or so of discussion about Peak Oil, or for that matter any other manifestation of the predicament of industrial civilization, and you'll find the climactic scenes of both stories—the basement entrepreneur laboring away at the technological fix that will save us all, on the one hand, and the plucky band of survivors blasting away with assault rifles at savage, starving, mindless mobs, on the other—circling like broken records.

I've come to think that much of the mutual incomprehension that strangles communication among different sides of the Peak Oil scene, and has played an important part in keeping it fragmented and marginalized, comes from the way that so many people in that scene have their ears so full of one or another of these stories that they can't hear anything else. Still, these two aren't the only stories that have had this kind of effect on the debate, and I'd like to talk a little bit about one of the others in this week's post. The story in question is at least as old as the other two, and it has, if anything, even more pervasive a presence in the rhetoric that shapes our collective thinking about the future. Call it the story of the eleventh hour.

You know that story inside and out already. It's the one in which the world is on the brink of disaster, for some simple and readily defined reason that could be solved if people were only willing to do what was necessary. Things get worse, and worse, and worse, until at the last possible moment before disaster strikes—at the eleventh hour, to use the constantly repeated phrase—people leap up from their sofas and do whatever it is that they have to do to save the world. A few cautionary words about being more proactive next time rounds off the story, and then they all live happily ever after.

It's a whacking good yarn, of course, which accounts for much of its popularity—everyone likes a taut suspenseful tale—and, like the other narratives we use these days to make sense of the future, it can be applied to almost any situation you care to name. It's also a very politically useful story, which accounts for the other half of its popularity. If you can convince people that the world really is on the brink of disaster, it's a good deal easier to stampede them into action, and if you can present them with a plan of action you claim will save the world, people may not look at the details too closely before they embrace it as their one hope of salvation. This can be exceedingly useful, particularly if you have an agenda your audience might not support if they know they have another choice.

The last three hundred years or so of North American cultural politics are full of individuals and movements who discovered these advantages in the story of the Eleventh Hour. One of the most relevant is also one of the earliest. I don't know if any of my readers were introduced in college literature classes, as I was, to Jonathan Edwards' harrowing 1741 sermon *Sinners in the Hands of an Angry God.* Like so many preachers before and since, Edwards faced the not inconsiderable challenge of convincing human beings to live like angels, and made the often repeated discovery that one of the best ways to do it was to scare the stuffing out of them. The result is one of the most spectacular invocations of the eleventh hour in all of literature. Edwards bent all his talents to the task of convincing his listeners that as they sat their in their pews, right then and there, the ground might suddenly open up beneath them and drop them screaming and flailing into the jaws of eternal damnation.

It was a great success at the time. Like so many preachers before and since, though, Edwards discovered the homely moral of the story of the boy who cried wolf: you can only scare the stuffing out of people in the same way so many times before the impact wears off, and your listeners become irritated or, worse yet, bored. Few things in popular culture have less cachet than last year's imminent disasters.

This is problematic for the Jonathan Edwardses of the world, who tend to be one-trick ponies, with careers founded on a single catastrophe and a solution to match. It can be even more problematic for the rest of us, though, because it does sometimes happen that one or more of the Jonathan Edwardses of an age proclaim a disaster that actually is in the offing—even a broken clock is right twice a day—and the story of the boy who cried wolf has two additional morals not often remembered: first, the wolves were real; second, they ended up eating the sheep.

That's the hidden downside of the story of the eleventh hour. When you've told the same story often enough, people become used to the fact that you'll be back again shortly with another catastrophe du jour, and another one after that, and so on. They stop being scared and become irritated or, worse yet, bored. At that point it doesn't matter how many more changes you ring on the story or how colorfully you describe this year's imminent disaster, because they've learned to recognize the narrative *as narrative*—and, not uncommonly, they've learned to glimpse whatever agenda lies behind the story and motivates the people who tell it.

The awkward conversation about Peak Oil in today's industrial societies, I'm convinced, cannot be understood at all unless the spreading effect of these paired recognitions is taken into account. For decades now our collective discourse has been filled to overflowing with competing renditions of the story of the eleventh hour, from every imaginable point on the political and cultural spectrum. Whether it's the missile gap or the ozone layer, fiat currencies or emerging viruses, immigration policy or trade deficits or the antics of whatever set of clowns is piling into or out of the executive branch this season, somebody or other is presenting it as a source of imminent disaster from which, at the eleventh hour, their proposals can save us.

This is the environment into which the Peak Oil movement emerged when it left its larval stage on a handful of internet mailing lists and started to try to warn the world that the age of cheap abundant energy is about to come to an end. In the language of theater, they found themselves playing to a very unsympathetic house. Mind you, it didn't help that a significant number of people in the Peak Oil community proceeded to pack their message into the familiar framework of the story of the eleventh hour, complete in many cases with unstated political agendas that are not unfamiliar to those of us who have watched the last thirty years' worth of imminent disasters come and go.

The irony here, and it's as rich as it is bitter, is that this is one of the cases where the crisis is real. Depending on how you measure it—with or without natural gas liquids, oil-sands products, and other marginal sources of quasipetroleum fuel—world oil production peaked in 2005 or 2006 and, despite record prices and massive drilling programs in the Middle East and elsewhere, has been slipping down the far side of Hubbert's peak ever since. Dozens of countries in the nonindustrial world are already struggling with desperate shortages of petroleum products, while the industrial world's attempts to stave off trouble by pouring its food supply into its gas tanks via ethanol and biodiesel have succeeded mostly in launching food prices on a stratospheric trajectory from which they show no signs of returning any time soon.

Does this mean that we're finally, for real, at the eleventh hour? That's the richest and most bitter irony of all. As Robert Hirsch and his colleagues pointed out not long ago in a crucial study, the only way to respond effectively to Peak Oil on a national scale, and stave off massive economic and social disruptions, is to start preparations twenty years before the arrival of peak petroleum production. The eleventh hour, in other words, came and went in 1986, and no amount of pressure, protest, or wishful thinking can make up for the opportunity that was missed then. Listen carefully today and you can hear the sound of the clock tolling twelve, reminding us that the eleventh hour is gone for good.

The problem with this realization, of course, is that the story of the twelfth hour doesn't make good melodrama. When you're standing in the train station watching the train you meant to catch rattling out of sight around a distant curve miles down the track, it's hard to capture the excitement of the desperate pelting run through the station that gets you onto the train just as it starts rolling toward the destination you hoped to reach. Equally, the story of the twelfth hour isn't all that useful as a tool of political manipulation, since the silence of an empty train station makes it rather too easy to stop and think about whether the destination you hoped to reach was actually someplace you wanted to go.

While it may not make good melodrama or effective politics, though, I've come to think that one of the things we most need just now, in the Peak Oil scene and in modern industrial civilization as a whole, is that time of reflection in the silence that follows when the eleventh hour has come and gone, and the last hope of avoiding the consequences of our actions has vanished down the track into the land of might-have-beens. It's been pointed out more than once that the process of coming to terms with Peak Oil has more than a little in common with the five stages of grief—denial, anger, bargaining, depression, and acceptance—that Elizabeth Kubler-Ross injected into our cultural dialogue and Cliff Gorman made famous in Bob Fosse's extraordinary movie *All That Jazz*. It's been noticed much less often that the final stage of the process has a gift to offer, and the name of the gift is wisdom—something the world arguably needs a good deal more than it needs another round of comforting melodrama, or another set of political agendas disguising themselves as solutions to yet another catastrophe du jour.

Arguments from Ignorance

(Originally published 29 October 2008)

For some time now I've been wondering how to bring up a certain habit of thought that, as I see it, forms one of the taproots feeding the contemporary crisis of industrial civilization. That it had to be discussed here on *The Archdruid Report* I never doubted, but in the midst of a cascade of dramatic current events, that discussion can seem very nearly beside the point. When the system of hallucinatory finance that propped up the illusion of American prosperity for a quarter century may be going to pieces around us, panic selling in commodity markets by speculators hit with margin calls is sending fossil fuel prices to lows just as unsustainable as their recent highs, and the wheels are coming off America's global empire, I find myself wondering, is it really a good time to go wandering off in pursuit of intangibles?

Then perspective returns, and I remember that it's precisely the intangibles, the states of mind and attitudes toward the world that form a culture's collective discourse, that define what it can and cannot accomplish as the age of oil comes to an end. As I've commented before, it's not technical issues that make our present predicament so difficult; it's the failure of collective will that keeps even the most grudging acknowledgment of our predicament, and even the most modest response to it, completely off the radar screens of mainstream politics in every nation in the industrial world. Until the "mind-forg'd manacles" of dysfunctional thinking are unlocked and tossed aside, constructive plans for the world after peak oil on anything past an individual level are wasted effort, since they will not be implemented by societies that cannot grasp the need for them.

I had a cogent reminder of this over the past week, when three efforts of mine to spark collective discussion about these issues—my book *The Long Descent*, a reading and booksigning at a local bookstore here in southern Oregon, and the most recent post here— fielded three responses that used very different arguments to make a common claim. A reader of my book emailed me to tell me he thought I was refusing to give proper weight to the possibility that new technology would save our civilization from the impact of peak oil; a serious young man who attended the reading came up afterwards to ask me what I thought about the possibility that the current crisis would drive humanity to achieve a new stage of spiritual evolution, after which we will easily replace fossil fuels with currently unimaginable resources; a new reader of this blog sent in a comment insisting that peak oil was an illusion manufactured by sinister elites who were suppressing inventions that would allow everyone to have all the energy they wanted.

Mind you, I'd encountered every one of these assertions before. Ever since this blog first started suggesting that the end of the age of cheap abundant energy was the natural and inevitable result of a human ecology hopelessly out of step with the realities of life on a finite planet, I've fielded a great many emails and comments insisting, basically, that it just ain't so—that one way or another, for one reason or another, humanity could have its abundant energy resources and burn them too, and can reasonably expect more of the same forever. The three responses I've just cited by no means exhaust the full spectrum of arguments advanced to back this curious claim, but they're good representative samples of the type.

Now it's possible to dispute each of these claims on their own terms, and I've done that more than once on this blog and elsewhere, but there's a very real extent to which this is a waste of breath. Each of them is what the old logicians used to call an argument from ignorance. They insist on the presence of a factor that can't be proved or disproved—a technological advance that hasn't happened yet, an allegedly imminent spiritual transformation that has to be taken on blind faith, or a conspiracy so secret and pervasive that it can manipulate everything we think we know about the world—to insist that we don't actually have to do anything about peak oil.

Such arguments prove nothing, of course; their only virtue is that they're impossible to disprove. I've come to think that this last detail is why they're so popular. It's a very charming social habit, dating back to the eighteenth century Enlightenment, to profess the belief that people come to decisions about the world by sitting down with the relevant facts, assessing them calmly, and then making a decision on that basis. I think most of us are aware, though, that few decisions are actually made this way; much more often, people start from the conclusion that appeals to their emotions and intuition, and then go looking for logical reasons to support the belief they've already chosen.

Most of the time, this is actually a good thing. Left to itself, the reasoning mind tends to run to extremes; it's because most human decisions obey the nonrational promptings of emotional patterns laid down in childhood that our lives have any continuity at all. This same process, averaged out over the millions who inhabit a nation, provides a sense of stability and identity essential to our collective life. Still, the emotions' habit of projecting the past onto the blank screen of the future can become a ghastly liability when the future no longer resembles the past in some crucial sense.

That's the situation we're facing now. Between 1980 and 2005, political gimmickry and the reckless overproduction of the North Slope and North Sea oil fields crashed the price of oil to right around US$10 a barrel—corrected for inflation, the cheapest price in history. During that quarter century of unsustainable excess, energy was so cheap that the cost no longer mattered, it seemed to make perfect sense to live in rural Oregon and commute daily by jet to San Francisco or Seattle, or to arbitrage wage costs by manufacturing consumer goods for the American market in Third World sweatshops and shipping them halfway around the world to their customers, or to build internet server farms, thousands of them, each one drawing as much electricity from the grid as a medium-sized town.

That world of unlimited free energy is the world in which nearly all of us in the industrial world lived until very recently, and it's the only world people who are under the age of 35 or so can remember at all. Thus it's not surprising that when people are faced with the claim that the future will be very, very different, they tend to reject the notion out of hand, and if the only reasons they can find to justify that rejection are arguments from ignorance like the ones I cited above, then arguments from ignorance are what they'll cite.

The problem is that at this point we don't have time to wait for hypothetical solutions to show up and save us. The Hirsch Report pointed out in 2005 that, to avoid severe economic disruption, any effective response to peak oil had to get started at least twenty years before the beginning of petroleum production declines. Any less than that, and the result is damage to the economy; the shorter the lead time, the worse the damage, and waiting until production declines actually begin is a recipe for crippling economic impacts that could make it impossible to respond to the crisis effectively at all.

This is dire news, because we no longer have the twenty years Hirsch specified; we most likely have only two years left.[*] By most calculations, in fact, conventional petroleum production actually peaked the same year the Hirsch Report was published; apparent increases since then have happened because biofuels, tar sand extractives, and other alternative fuels that require high energy

---

[*] This estimate turned out to be inaccurate, of course; the hydrofracturing ("fracking") boom, which is unraveling as I write this, postponed the beginning of actual production declines for several more years.

inputs have been lumped together with conventional oil; and the best estimates suggest that even with the alternatives factored in, production will face serious declines beginning around 2010. That gives us desperately little time to respond, and no time to spare for arguments that insist some unknown phenomenon will pop out of the woodwork just in time to save us.

There are times late at night when I find myself wondering if similar reasonings could have been heard in the Yucatan lowlands as the Terminal Classic period of Mayan history arrived. and the paired jaws of declining soil fertility and catastrophic drought clamped around the throat of Lowland Maya civilization. There were plenty of potential responses as the corn harvests began to fail, centering on a transition from corn culture to less valued foods such as ramon nuts, but ideological factors made such a transition difficult for the *ahauob*, "divine lords" of the Maya city-states, to contemplate; abundant corn harvests filled the same role in their culture as abundant fossil fuel supplies have in ours.

Thus, instead of facing the crisis, the *ahauob* responded by hoping that something would provide them with a way out of it. Some of them, anticipating America's recent neoconservative movement, went to war with other city-states to seize their corn supplies, while others offered up human sacrifices and built ever more grandiose temples in the hopes that the gods would take the crisis away. None of this helped, and much of it probably made the situation worse; one way or another, the result was a "rolling collapse" that, over a century and a half, turned the thriving Maya cities of the lowlands to crumbling, overgrown ruins inhabited by a scattering of survivors.

The idea that the cities of contemporary North America could meet the same fate is quite literally unthinkable to most people today, but then the Maya, the Romans, and the people of other collapsed civilizations all probably found their historical destiny just as unthinkable before it happened. There may be little reason to hope that anything like a majority can be helped to think the unthinkable in time to make a difference, but the effort seems worth making, and challenging the sort of arguments from ignorance I've described above might be a good first step.

The Pornography
of Political Fear
(Originally published 21 January 2009)

In most respects, despite the media hoopla, yesterday was an ordinary day. Amid brisk January weather, one of the world's large nations marked the installation of a new chief executive with the usual round of ceremonies and celebrations. The transition was orderly to the point of dullness; the retiring president and his replacement had coffee together in the White House before the ceremony, and afterwards walked together with every evidence of cordiality to the helicopter that would ferry one of them back into private life.

I am not sure how many people noticed that the clatter of rotor blades as that helicopter took off put a period at the end of some of the most extravagant rhetoric of the Bush era. For the past eight years, a great many voices had insisted that the weary Texan who left the White House yesterday was about to declare martial law, suspend the Constitution, cancel all future elections, order dissidents to be rounded up and interned in concentration camps built by Halliburton, and a great deal more of the same kind. If, dear reader, you were one of the people who spent George W. Bush's presidential terms insisting that these things were about to happen, grab a beer from the fridge and have a seat, because we need to talk.

The rumors I've just described were very nearly an article of faith across large sectors of the American left in the years just past. Hundreds of websites and a sizeable number of talk radio programs presented them as matters of simple fact, and vied with one another to accuse the Bush administration of the most diabolical intentions. Those who pointed out that the purveyors of these ideas never quite got around to offering the least scrap of evidence to back them tended to be dismissed with scorn. Yet the fact remains that all those claims were quite simply wrong.

It's a bit uncomfortable to be the one who points this out, because I am no fan of George W. Bush. I voted against him in two elections, and have never regretted either vote. He and the neoconservative movement that used him as its sock puppet did a great deal to damage the country I love. Yet it's always seemed to me that a person should be criticized for the things he does, not the intentions that his worst enemies impute to him. Bush was certainly a bad president; he may even, as many of those enemies have claimed, be a bad person. Somehow, though, it seems to have been forgotten that these points do not justify telling lies about him.

The enthusiasm with which those rumors were minted and spread is all the more ironic, in that some of the people who participated most eagerly were among those who complained bitterly when right-wing pundits and websites meted out the same treatment to Bill Clinton during the latter's two terms. I think most of us who were around at that time heard more than our fill about UN troop convoys rolling down American highways, black helicopters crisscrossing the skies, and Clinton's personal plan to put America under the yoke of a tyrannical world government that would send gun owners and evangelical Christians to concentration camps. Those stories were just as unsupported by evidence and disproven by events as the equivalent claims about Bush, or the flurry of similar stories already beginning to circulate about President Obama.

The last two decades, in fact, have seen the rise of what might best be called a pornography of political fear in America's collective discourse. Like other forms of pornography, it flattens the rich complexity of human interaction into a one-dimensional world in which abstract shapes and motions stimulate unthinking reactions from the brainstem levels of its viewers. It thus debases what it claims to describe, even as it pursues whatever raw sensation it evokes further and further away from any human reality. The payoff of the pornography of political fear is different from the one experienced by those who have their hands down inside some less metaphorical pair of shorts, but it is every bit as reflexive, and its results can be just as messy.

The nature of that payoff deserves some discussion here. Hate in contemporary America has much the same status given to some other words with four letters in earlier times: a great many people affect to despise it, and condemn those who practice it publicly, while thirsting for the chance to engage in it themselves. The pornography of political fear appeals precisely because it provides a culturally sanctioned opportunity to indulge in the forbidden pleasures of unrestrained hate. The intoxication of feeling justified, and even virtuous, while wallowing in hatred for an irredeemably evil Other is a potent force in today's culture—and it may yet become an equally powerful factor in tomorrow's politics, with disastrous results.

An earlier post on this blog explored the way that terms such as "fascist" have been stripped of their contexts and turned into all-purpose epithets with no other meaning beyond "I hate you." This common pattern of rhetoric makes it difficult to draw any useful lesson from the bitter history of twentieth century totalitarian governments, but the effort needs to be made, because certain features of contemporary culture display unwelcome similarities to the conditions that helped those earlier nightmares claw their way into waking life.

One of them is precisely this habit of allowing pornographic fantasies of political evil to pass unchallenged as reasonable discourse. In the decades leading up to the rise of European fascism

In the 1920s and 1930s, rhetoric no more heated than today's torrents of partisan vilification spread through all sides of the political controversies of the day. This did much to create an atmosphere of collective hatred in which it no longer seemed unreasonable, to far too many people, to single out one group within society as the source of all its problems—and set out to remove those problems by exterminating their supposed source.

More than two thousand years ago, much the same process was mapped out in precise detail by a long line of Greek philosophers, who explored the ways that the republics of the classical world gave way to tyranny. The key to the process, according to many of these ancient witnesses, was the rise of bitter factional struggles over wealth and power that spun so far out of hand that the machinery of civil government broke apart and the rule of a tyrant became the only alternative to chaos and civil war. In a nation where a noticeable number of members of either party don't seem to be able to walk past a picture of the other party's candidate without screaming obscenities at it, we are closer to that outcome than most people realize.

Such habits flourish these days because representative democracy has always been an easy target for its critics. Abuses of power and displays of rank incompetence happen in democracies and closed societies alike, but in democracies they are more likely to become public knowledge and can be denounced in comparative safety—those people who fling the word "fascist" at today's democracies, for example, can do so without having to worry in the least about being dragged from their beds in the middle of the night by armed men in jackboots and hauled away to a prison camp. Since politics in a representative democracy requires a constant process of compromise among competing pressure groups and power centers, furthermore, it's rare for any side to get everything it wants, and this breeds dissatisfaction with the system.

That in itself is no vice—reasoned dissent is the lifeblood of a republic—but when dissatisfaction festers into the insistence that one's own side ought always to get everything it wants, and the habit of demonizing the other side for standing up for its own interests and hopes for the future, something has gone terribly wrong. It may be one of the bitterest ironies of the next few decades that those who label their political enemies as fascists, by that very act, are helping to build a climate of political hatred, and contempt for flawed but functioning democracies, that could make something like fascism inevitable in today's America—and a future totalitarian state, it bears remembering, could as easily arise from today's political left wing as from the right.

It may already be too late to avoid that experience. Still, the effort is worth making, and one place to start is a principled rejection of the pornography of political fear. So, dear reader, when somebody tells you that Barack Obama is personally plotting to enslave you— and you will hear that claim in the near future, if you have not heard it already[*]—I suggest that at the very least, you ask for some evidence more convincing than the splutterings of a fringe media personality or a conspiracy theory website that made exactly the same claims about Clinton and Bush. If we are going to get through the unraveling of industrial civilization with anything like a functioning society, the bad habits of rejecting the claims of a common humanity, demonizing political disagreement, and projecting the shadows of our own frustrations and failures onto the faces of our political enemies, are luxuries we can no longer afford.

---

[*] I admit that even I was surprised at the level of vituperation and the bizarre paralogic with which this prediction was fulfilled.

A Deindustrial Reading List
(Originally published 4 February 2009)

Over the last few months a number of people have asked me what books I think they ought to read to help them prepare for the slow unraveling of industrial civilization now getting started around us. This is frankly the kind of question I try my best to dodge. Premature consensus is arguably one of the most severe risks we face just now, and any image of the future—very much including the one I've sketched out here—is at best a scattershot sampling of the divergent possibilities facing us as the industrial age comes to its end.

Thus anything that tends to encourage people in the peak oil movement, or the wider society around it, to think about the future in any stereotyped way is potentially fatal. Still, several readers have noted that the ideas in my book *The Long Descent* and these essays presuppose a worldview and a cultural and intellectual inheritance that aren't exactly widespread in popular culture these days. They've asked, if I may paraphrase a bit, what they should read to make better sense of my ravings. Put that way, it's not an unreasonable request, and since the view of history that shapes those ravings flies in the face of most of the common assumptions of the modern world, a little background may not hurt.

I've thus sketched out a reading list of sorts for those interested in exploring in more detail the viewpoint I've presented here. It contains nearly as many broad categories as specific book recommendations; I have my preferences, and will suggest them, but here again diversity of opinion and information are essential. If everybody in your neighborhood reads and uses the techniques in a different gardening book, the resulting knowledge base will be much larger and more useful than if everybody relies on a single text, with its inevitable omissions and errors.

For similar reasons, most of the books mentioned below are relatively old, and some of them are out of print. There are excellent new books on most of these subjects, and I certainly encourage you to read as many of those as appeal to you, but books written during any historical period mirror that period's presuppositions and habits of thought to a much greater extent than anybody notices at the time. One advantage of older books is precisely that their unthinking assumptions are easier to catch, and this in turn helps foster the awkward but essential realization that thirty years from now, the unquestioned truths and apparently reasonable assumptions of the present will look as outlandishly dated as bell bottom pants and disco music.

Very few of the books I've suggested here are practical, in any ordinary sense of the word, and those that have that distinction are meant to be read and interpreted in rather impractical ways. The sheer diversity of potentials and needs that will likely open up in a deindustrializing future makes any sort of practical booklist an exercise in overgeneralization; the entire thrust of the deindustrial age heads from standardized approaches toward the diversity that comes from a renewed engagement with the local realities of one's own place, time, and community. A reader whose future career involves raising draft horses in rural Iowa has completely different practical needs from a reader who, ten years from now, will be salvaging and repairing appliances in a small West Coast city; what they need in common is a framework of ideas that will help them make sense of the wider picture, and the ideas I am trying to explore here provide one of these.

Finally, I've made some suggestions about how to approach the books mentioned below. At the risk of sounding like a 19th-century schoolmaster, I probably need to point out that you won't get much out of any book if you approach it passively, and let the words dribble through your mind and out your ears like so many sitcom plots. The books I've suggested are not there so that you can agree with them unthinkingly; they are meant to get you to look under the hood of the ideas I've offered and see how the machinery works.

With those caveats, here goes. The following books should be read, if you can manage that, in the order I've listed them.

1. A basic textbook of ecology. It really doesn't matter which one; the two on my bookshelves are Richard Brewer's *Principles of Ecology* and Eugene P. Odum's *Fundamentals of Ecology*, but that's simply because these were the college textbooks I studied back in the day. What's essential is that the book you read should be a general textbook of scientific ecology, not a popularization or a polemic. A great many people have embraced ecology as an ideology or a sentimental pose without ever getting around to learning how living things and their environments interact. In the future, I'm convinced, a clear and unsentimental understanding of the way ecology works will be the most essential branch of human knowledge, and could spare individuals and communities some bitter lessons in the years to come. A basic grasp of ecology is also essential for making sense of the next three books.

2. *The Limits to Growth* by Donella Meadows, Dennis Meadows, Jorgen Randers, and William W. Behrens III. Get the original 1972 edition rather than either of the two updates, in which the original message has been partly overlaid with political polemic. The most insightful and thus inevitably the most vilified of the 1970s collapse literature, *The Limits to Growth* was the first book I know of to point out the central paradox of a perpetual growth economy: if economic growth is pursued far enough, the costs of further growth begin to rise faster than its benefits, and eventually force the growth economy to its knees. Joseph Tainter's *The Collapse of Complex Societies* explored the same territory later on from another angle, and my essay on catabolic collapse did the same thing from a different angle again; still, the original presentation remains the most useful. Note whether *The Limits to Growth* makes more or less sense in the light of the basic ecological principles you read in the first book.

3. *Overshoot* by William R. Catton Jr. Still far and away the best book on the twilight of the age of cheap energy, *Overshoot* is also one of the very few explorations of that troubling territory that is fully grounded in a clear grasp of ecological realities. A good half of the ideas explored in *The Archdruid Report* can trace their origins to one page or another of Catton's book. It is challenging reading and, in many places, depressing as well; Catton resolutely refuses to offer easy answers for the predicament into which industrial society has backed itself. Of all the currently out-of-print books on this list, though, this is the one I would most like to see reissued by some small publisher. Once again, assess Catton's claims in the light of the basic ecological principles you've learned.

4. A practical introduction to intensive organic gardening. John Jeavons' *How To Grow More Vegetables* and John Seymour's *The Self-Sufficient Gardener* are among the examples on my shelves (along with a number of more recent books, of course). It's best to choose one you haven't read before. The goal here is not to learn how to grow food using intensive organic methods—though that's very likely a good idea—but rather to think through the practical implications of the ecological ideas you've just studied. Ask yourself where the system of gardening presented by the book you're reading works with ecological cycles, and where it conflicts with them; imagine ways in which the logic governing organic gardening could be applied to other aspects of society and economy, and try to get a sense of the costs and benefits of making a transition from current practices to the ones you've imagined.

5 and 6. *The Decline of the West* by Oswald Spengler and *A*

Study of History by **Arnold Toynbee.** Get the abridged edition of each; the complete two-volume Spengler is hard to get, and only obsessive history fans like me work their way through all twelve volumes of Toynbee, but the one-volume Spengler abridgment and either the two-volume or the later one-volume versions of Toynbee are cheap, readily available, and no great challenge to read. These are the two great modern presentations of the case for cyclic history; they cover much the same territory, but each one does it from a unique perspective. Read them close together, and notice the places where Toynbee is arguing with Spengler's theories and conclusions; the Great Conversation is rarely quite so audible as here. While you read both books, notice whether the ecological perspectives you've absorbed from the first three books cast any additional light on the cycles outlined by these two authors.

7. The history of a dead civilization. It doesn't matter which one, and you have plenty of options to choose from. The only requirements are that the civilization should be as extinct as a dodo; the book you choose should focus on history rather than culture— that is, it should talk about what events happened in what order, rather than simply wallowing in the cultural high points and quietly neglecting how things fell to bits thereafter; and it should cover the whole history of the civilization from its origin to its collapse. As you trace the rise and fall of the civilization you've chosen, bring the lessons of the first six books to bear on it. What role did ecological factors in general, and the specific problems traced by Meadows et al. and Catton, play in your civilization's rise and fall? How well do Spengler's and Toynbee's accounts of historical change fit the facts in this specific case?

8. *Muddling Toward Frugality* by Warren Johnson. This one may be a challenge to find; it appeared right at the end of the 1970s, had a brief flurry of popularity, and then vanished without a trace in the wave of reaction that swept Ronald Reagan into the White House and the lessons of the previous decade into oblivion. Regardless, it's one of the most thoughtful works to come out of the last energy crisis, an argument for unplanned, undramatic, and thoroughly non-ideological change as the best option at the end of the Age of Abundance. Johnson's analysis is much subtler than it looks; this is another book that needs to get back in print sooner rather than later. While reading it, bring your previous reading to bear on it; in particular, ask yourself how useful its proposals would have been if implemented at various points in the decline and fall of the civilization you studied.

9. *Where The Wasteland Ends* by Theodore Roszak. A brilliant, engaging, frustrating work, this is Roszak's exploration of the narratives and assumptions about reality that undergird modern industrial civilization. Some of my readers will find its argument appealing, while others will find it intolerable; both groups stand to learn a great deal from this book if they set aside these emotional reactions and pay attention to the way that Roszak crafts his case, to his choice of examples and evidence, and also to the things he doesn't address. As you read it, put it in its historical context: if it had been written in a dead civilization just before decline set in, what would Spengler and Toynbee have said about it? Then take it out of its historical context: what does its argument have to offer us now?

10. A book predicting a dramatic social transformation that didn't happen. Choose one that you would have rooted for at the time. If you believe that civilization is the root of all evils, pick up the sturdy Victorian radical Edward Carpenter's *Civilization: Its Cause and Cure*; if you believe that we are on the verge of breakthrough into a new kind of consciousness, try Charles Reich's *The Greening of America*; if you're secretly hoping for social collapse and mass dieoff, read one of the hundreds of books that have been predicting exactly that for the last dozen centuries, and so on. Try to put yourself into the mindset of the readers who believed it when it first saw print; see why it seemed to make sense at the time – and then step back and explore the reasons why nothing of the sort actually happened. Bring everything you've learned from the previous nine books to bear on this one.

There you have it. It would probably be possible to draw up a list of books in print that would cast the same light on the ideas I'm trying to explore here. It would also be possible to draw up a list drawn entirely from Greek and Roman classical authors—though this would take a tolerance for the sort of thinking modern people mislabel "mysticism" well beyond what most readers have nowadays. Still, this is my list, and I'm stickin' with it; those who tackle it, on the off chance that anybody does, will end up with a much clearer idea of what I'm trying to say in these essays, and with any luck, will be able to go further with these curious notions than I have.

The Onset of
Catabolic Collapse
(Originally published 11 January 2011)

I've commented more than once in these essays on the gap in perception between history as it appears in textbooks and history as it's lived by people on the spot at the time. That's a gap worth watching, because the foreshortening of history that comes with living in the middle of it quite often gets in the way of figuring out a useful response to a time of crisis—for example, the one we're in right now.

This is all the more challenging because the foreshortening of history cuts both ways; it makes small but sudden events look more important than they are, and it also helps hide slow but massive shifts that will play a much greater role in shaping the future. Recent increases in the price of oil, for example, kicked off a flurry of predictions suggesting that hyperinflation and the sudden collapse of industrial society are right around the corner; identical predictions were made the last time oil prices spiked, the time before that, and the time before that, too, so the traditional grain of salt may be worth adding to them this time around. (We'll most likely get hyperinflation in the US, granted, but my guess is that that will come further down the road.) Look at all these price spikes and notice that the peaks and troughs have both tended gradually upwards, on the other hand, and you may just catch sight of the signal hidden in all that noise—the fact that providing industrial civilization with its most important fuel is loading a greater burden on the world's economies with every year that passes.

The same gap in perception afflicts most current efforts to make sense of the future looming up ahead of us. Ever since my original paper on catabolic collapse first found its way onto the internet, I've fielded questions fairly regularly from people who want to know whether I think some current or imminent crisis will tip industrial society over into catabolic collapse in some unmistakably catastrophic way. It's a fair question, but it's based on a fundamental misreading both of the concept of catabolic collapse and of our present place in the long cycles of rise and fall that define the history of civilizations.

Let's start with some basics, for the sake of those of my readers who haven't waded their way through the fine print of the paper.[*] The central idea of catabolic collapse is that human societies pretty consistently tend to produce more stuff than they can afford to maintain. What we are pleased to call "primitive societies"—that is, societies that are well enough adapted to their environments that they get by comfortably without huge masses of cumbersome and expensive infrastructure – usually do so in a fairly small way, and very often evolve traditional ways of getting rid of excess goods at regular intervals so that the cost of maintaining it doesn't become a burden. As societies expand and start to depend on complex infrastructure to support the daily activities of their inhabitants, though, it becomes harder and less popular to do this, and so the maintenance needs of the infrastructure and the rest of the society's stuff gradually build up until they reach a level that can't be covered by the resources on hand.

It's what happens next that's crucial to the theory. The only

---

[*] "How Civilizations Fall: A Theory of Catabolic Collapse" was originally published on the internet in 2005, and has since been republished as an appendix to my book *The Long Descent*.

40

reliable way to solve a crisis that's caused by rising maintenance costs is to cut those costs, and the most effective way of cutting maintenance needs is to tip some fraction of the stuff that would otherwise have to be maintained into the nearest available dumpster. That's rarely popular, and many complex societies resist it as long as they possibly can, but once it happens the usual result is at least a temporary resolution of the crisis. Now of course the normal human response to the end of a crisis is the resumption of business as usual, which in the case of a complex society generally amounts to amassing more stuff. Thus the normal rhythm of history in complex societies cycles back and forth between building up, or anabolism, and breaking down, or catabolism. Societies that have been around a while—China comes to mind—have cycled up and down through this process dozens of times, with periods of prosperity and major infrastructure projects alternating with periods of impoverishment and infrastructure breakdown.

A more dramatic version of the same process happens when a society is meeting its maintenance costs with nonrenewable resources. If the resource is abundant enough – for example, the income from a global empire, or half a billion years of ancient sunlight stored underground in the form of fossil fuels—and the rate at which it's extracted can be increased over time, at least for a while, a society can heap up unimaginable amounts of stuff without worrying about the maintenance costs. The problem, of course, is that neither imperial expansion nor fossil fuel drawdown can keep on going indefinitely on a finite planet. Sooner or later you run into the limits of growth; at that point the costs of keeping wealth flowing in from your empire or your oil fields begin a ragged but unstoppable increase, while the return on that investment begins an equally ragged and equally unstoppable decline; the gap between your maintenance needs and available resources spins out of control, until your society no longer has enough resources on hand even to provide for its own survival, and it goes under.

That's catabolic collapse. It's not quite as straightforward as it sounds, because each burst of catabolism on the way down does lower maintenance costs significantly, and can also free up resources for other uses. The usual result is the stairstep sequence of decline that's traced by the history of so many declining civilizations—half a century of crisis and disintegration, say, followed by several decades of relative stability and partial recovery, and then a return to crisis; rinse and repeat, and you've got the process that turned the Forum of imperial Rome into an early medieval sheep pasture.

It's easy enough to track catabolic collapse at work in retrospect, when you can glance over a couple of centuries of decline in an evening with one of Michael Grant's excellent histories of Rome in one hand and a glass of decent bourbon in the other. Catching it in process, though, can be a much more challenging task, because it happens on a scale considerably larger than a human lifespan. In its early stages, the signal is hard to tease out from ordinary economic and political fluctuations; later on, it's all too easy to believe that any given period of stabilization has solved the problem, at least until the next wave of crises rolls in; late in the game, as crisis piles on top of crisis and cracks are opening up everywhere, your society's glory days are so far in the past that it's surprisingly easy to lose track of the fact that calamity isn't the normal shape of things.

Still, the attempt is worth making, and I propose to make it here. In fact, I'd like to suggest that it's possible at this point to provide a fairly exact date for the onset of catabolic collapse here in the United States of America.

That America is a prime candidate for catabolic collapse seems tolerably clear at this point, though I'm sure plenty of people can find reasons to argue with that assessment. It's considered impolite to talk about America's empire nowadays, but the US troops currently garrisoned in 140 countries around the world are not there for their health, after all, and it requires a breathtaking suspension of disbelief to insist that this global military presence has nothing to do with the fact that the 5% of our species that live in this country use around a quarter of the world's total energy production and around a third of its raw materials and industrial products. The United States has an empire, then, and it's become an extraordinarily expensive empire to maintain; the fact that the US spends as much money on its military annually as all the other nations on Earth put together is only one measure of the maintenance cost involved.

That America is also irrevocably committed to dependence on dwindling supplies nonrenewable fossil fuels also seems clear at this point, though here again there are plenty who would dispute the point. Even if there were other energy resources available in the same gargantuan amounts—and despite decades of enthusiastic claims, every attempt to deploy other energy resources to replace a significant amount of fossil fuels has run headfirst into crippling problems of scale—the political will to carry out a transition soon enough to matter has not been present, and the careful analyses in the 2005 Hirsch report are among the many good reasons for thinking that the window of opportunity for that transition is long past. The notion that America can drill its way out of crisis would be funny if the situation was not so serious; despite dizzyingly huge government subsidies and the best oil exploration and extraction technology on Earth, US oil production has been in decline since 1972. As the first nation to develop a commercial petroleum industry, it was probably inevitable that we would be among the very first to hit the limits to production and begin slipping down the arc of decline. As for coal and natural gas, the abundance of the former and the glut of the latter are the product of short term factors; while press releases aimed mostly at boosting stock prices insist that we'll have supplies of both for centuries to come, more sober analysts have gotten past the hype and the hugely inflated reserve figures and predicted hard peaks for both fuels within thirty years, and quite possibly sooner.

That being the case, the question is simply when to place the first wave of catabolism in America—the point at which crises bring a temporary end to business as usual, access to real wealth becomes a much more challenging thing for a large fraction of the population, and significant amounts of the national infrastructure are abandoned or stripped for salvage. It's not a difficult question to answer, either.

The date in question is 1974.

That was the year when the industrial heartland of the United States, a band of factories that reached from Pennsylvania and upstate New York straight across to Indiana and Michigan, began its abrupt transformation into the Rust Belt. Hundreds of thousands of factory jobs, the bread and butter of America's then-prosperous working class, went away forever, and state and local governments went into a fiscal tailspin that saw many basic services cut to the bone and beyond. Meanwhile, wild swings in markets for agricultural commodities and fossil fuels, worsened by government policy, pushed most of rural America into a depression from which it has never recovered. In the terms I've suggested in this post, the US catabolized most of its heavy industry, most of its family farms, and a good half or so of its working class, among other things. It also set in motion the process of catabolizing one of the most important resources it had left at that time, the oil reserves of the Alaska North Slope. That oil could have been eked out over decades to cushion the transition to a low-energy future; instead, it was pumped and burnt at a breakneck pace in order to deal with the immediate crisis.

The United States was not alone in embracing catabolism in the mid-1970s. Britain abandoned most of its own heavy industry at the same time, plunging large parts of the industrial Midlands and Scotland into permanent depression, and set about catabolizing its own North Sea oil reserves with the same misplaced enthusiasm that American politicians lavished on the North Slope. The result was exactly what history would suggest; by embracing catabolism, the US and Britain both staggered through the crisis years of the 1970s and came out the other side into a breathing space of relative stability in the Reagan and Thatcher years,. That breathing space was extended significantly when the collapse of the Eastern Bloc, beginning in 1989, allowed American and British economic interests and their local surrogates to snap up wealth across Eurasia for pennies on the hundred-dollar bill, in the process imposing the same sort of economic collapse on most of a continent that had previously been inflicted on the steelworkers of Pittsburgh and the shipbuilders of Glasgow.

That breathing space ended in 2008. At this point, I'd suggest, we're in the early stages of a second and probably more severe round of catabolism here in America, and throughout Europe as well. What happened to the industrial working class in the 1970s is now happening to a very broad swath of the middle class, as jobs evaporate, public services are slashed, and half a dozen states stumble down the slope that will turn them into the Rust Belt equivalents of the early 21st century. Exactly what will happen as that process continues is anybody's guess, but it's unlikely to end as soon as the round of catabolism in the 1970s, and it may very well cut deeper; neither we nor Britain nor any other of our close allies has a big new petroleum reserve just waiting to be tapped, after all.

It's crucial to remember, though, that catabolism is a response to crisis and at least in the short term, much more often than not, an effective response. The fact that we're moving into the second stage of our society's long descent into catabolic collapse doesn't mean that America will fall apart in the next decade or so; quite the contrary, it strongly suggests that America will *not* fall apart this time around. As the current round of catabolism picks up speed, a great many jobs will go away, and most of them will never return; a great many people who depend on those jobs will descend into poverty, and most of them will never rise back out of it; much of the familiar fabric of life in America as it's been lived in recent decades will be shredded beyond repair, and new and far less lavish patterns will emerge instead; outside the narrowing circle of the privileged classes, even those who maintain relative affluence will be making do with much less than they or their equivalents do today. All these are ways that a society in decline successfully adapts to the contraction of its economic base and the mismatch between available resources and maintenance costs.

Twenty or thirty or forty years from now, in turn, it's a fairly safe bet that the years of crisis will come to a close and a newly optimistic America will reassure itself that everything really is all right again. The odds are pretty high that by then it will be, for all practical purposes, a Third World nation, with little more than dim memories remaining from its former empire or its erstwhile status as a superpower; it's not at all impossible, for that matter, that it will be more than one nation, split asunder along lines traced out by today's increasingly uncompromising culture wars. Fast forward another few decades, and another round of crises arrives, followed by another respite, and another round of crises, until finally peasant farmers plow their fields in sight of the crumbling ruins of our cities.

That's the way civilizations end, and that's the way ours is ending. The phrasing is deliberate: "is ending," not "will end." If I'm right, we're already half a lifetime into the decline and fall of industrial civilization. It can be challenging to keep that awareness in mind when wrestling with the day to day details of getting by in an ailing, sclerotic nation with a half-failed economy – or, for that matter, when trying out some of the technologies and tricks I've been discussing here in recent months. Still, it's worth making the attempt, because the wider view arguably makes it a bit easier to keep current events in perspective and plan for the future in which we will all, after all, be spending the rest of our lives.

Alternatives to Nihilism

(Three-part post, originally published 13, 20, and 27 April 2011)

Part One: A Dog Named Boo

"Where do you get your ideas?" is a question that most writers fairly often field, and generally dread. Science fiction writer Harlan Ellison is just about the only person in print with a ready answer; he used to state crisply—for all I know, he still does—that a little old lady in Poughkeepsie, New York sends him a weekly manila envelope full of story ideas. The rest of us are left to fumble with the difficult task of explaining the tangled roots of creativity.

Still, there are times when it's an easy question to answer, and for me, at least, this week is one of those. The idea behind this *Archdruid Report* post came from a comment on last week's post. My post was a comparison of today's vacuous political rhetoric on energy with the more pragmatic and effective responses that were pioneered during the energy crisis of the Seventies. The comment in its entirety—I've taken the liberty of adding such old-fashioned conveniences as capitals and punctuation—was this: "The days of 'Me and You and a Dog Named Boo' are over."

To some extent, that was simply another example of the sort of internet witticism that's designed to score points instead of addressing an argument. Equally, it's a fine example of unintentional irony, since the Seventies hit it referenced[*] was an open-road song that celebrated the freedom that cheap abundant petroleum briefly gave to footloose young Americans. In that sense, the comment is quite correct; the days of "another tank of gas and then back on the road again," to quote the song, are over for good.

Still, that wasn't what my commenter was saying, of course. What he or she was suggesting was that the conservation and alternative-energy technologies I discussed in last week's post were the products of an aspect of American popular culture that flourished in the Seventies, and died a wretched death in the decades that followed. The homebuilt solar panels, hand-typed guides to insulation and weatherstripping, basement-workshop inventions, lively little nonprofits running on raw enthusiasm and shoestring budgets, and the rest of the landscape of the Seventies appropriate-tech scene drew on the same cultural current that made "Me and You and a Dog Named Boo" a hit, and also, however briefly, had quite a few Americans thinking about living with a lot less energy and a lot fewer resources as an adventure rather than a fate worse than death.

It's easy to make fun of the excesses and eccentricities of the era: the air of well-scrubbed, fresh-faced innocence, say, that was so assiduously cultivated by the exact equivalents of those who now cultivate an equally artificial aura of sullen despair. Still, the 15% drop in America's petroleum consumption that took place between 1975 and 1985, coupled with equally sharp declines in other forms of energy use, might suggest that the John Denver fans of that time, with their granny glasses and dogs sporting brightly colored bandannas in place of collars, had something going for them that today's supposedly more sophisticated culture has not been able to match so far. The shift from the one to the other set of cultural themes may have more to do with that difference in outcomes than is

---

[*] The songs mentioned in each part of this post were hyperlinked in the blog to online music videos; since printed books don't have that feature, readers will have to arrange for their own soundtracks.

often recognized, and that possibility is one that needs to be explored.

That is to say, we need to talk about the roots of the contemporary American cult of nihilism.

I don't think that last phrase is too extreme a description. For the last few decades, it's been hugely fashionable in America to believe, or at least affect to believe, the cynical notions that all ideals are frauds or delusions, that those who try to live up to them are either posturing liars or simple-minded fools, and that we might as well enjoy ugliness because all beauty is by definition fake. Watching this week's idols dragged down to the lowest common denominator by yet another wretched scandal has become America's most popular spectator sport. Meanwhile, and crucially, the notion that the American people might face a challenge, any challenge, by rising to the occasion, much less might reasonably be encouraged to do so, gets dismissed out of hand by pundits, politicians, and ordinary people alike when it's mentioned at all. This wasn't always the case, and as this nation and the industrial world as a whole lurches blindly toward a set of challenges right up there with anything in the last five thousand years or so of recorded history, it bears asking why a rallying of the nation's will and potential that would have been an obvious part of a response to crisis fifty years ago is so unthinkable now.

It's useful, in making sense of this cultural shift, to remember that there are at least two kinds of cynicism. There's the kind—variously weary, amused, hurt, or icily dangerous—that comes naturally to those who have too often seen others betray their ideals. Then there's the other kind—sullen, jeering, brittle, and defensive—that comes just as naturally to those who betray their own ideals, and makes them lash out angrily whenever anything too reminiscent of that betrayal flicks them on the raw. It's the latter kind, I'm convinced, that shapes the mood of America today; the disquieting sounds that murmur through the crawlspaces of our collective imagination, waking us abruptly at night, are the echoes of a profoundly troubled national conscience.

For another measure of the same troubled conscience, think of the extraordinary reach of conspiracy theories of all kinds through American culture. These days, if you hear people talking about any of the problems or predicaments that beset our society, it's normally a safe bet that the conversation will end up fixating on some group of people whose monstrous wickedness is allegedly the cause of it all. Democrats talk that way about Republicans, and Republicans about Democrats, while those who have abandoned the grinning corpse of America's once-vital political culture have their own colorfully stocked rogues' galleries of alleged villains to offer.

Any of my readers who would like to see how much of this fixation on hunting for scapegoats unfolds from an uneasy conscience need only suggest in public that ordinary Americans might bear some modest degree of responsibility for the unwelcome trends of the last few decades. The shrillness with which most Americans will insist that all the blame lies elsewhere makes it tolerably clear just how sensitive a nerve has been touched. What Carl Jung called "projecting the shadow" has become a potent political reality in America, but you don't need a degree in Jungian psychoanalysis to realize that people who spend their lives pointing fingers at other people are trying to paste a villain's mask on the rest of the world in order to avoid seeing it when they look in the mirror.

A third measure? Consider the contemporary American obsession with apocalyptic fantasies. Back of all the gaudy claims of history's end currently on display—the Rapture, the Singularity, the supposed end of the Mayan calendar in 2012, and all the rest of it— is a frantic insistence that we don't have to live with the consequences of our collective actions. That's the common thread that connects the seeming optimism of the claim that Jesus or the Space Brothers or superintelligent computers will fix things, on the one hand, with the seeming pessimism of the claims that we're all about to be wiped out by solar flares or asteroid bombardment or the evil plans of the Illuminati. Either way, the world that our choices have made is not the world we have to inhabit; either way, it's not our responsibility to fix what we've broken, either because someone else is going to fix it or because it's all going to be blown to smithereens shortly by something that, please note, is never our fault.

All three of these factors have deep roots in American history, but it's not too hard to identify the point in time when they moved in from the fringes to dominate the collective imagination—and that lands us once again in the wake of the Seventies, the years when a society that previously idolized John-Boy Walton and John Denver suddenly started idolizing Gordon Gekko and self-proclaimed "material girl" Madonna instead.

Putting that shift into context requires a glance back over the history of the second half of the twentieth century. The aftermath of the Second World War left the United States abruptly filling the position of global hegemon previously held by Great Britain. In the aftermath of Hitler's defeat, Americans believed they had a permanent lease on the moral high ground as they expanded around the globe and confronted the Soviet Union. Mixed motives and the pressures of expediency had their usual effect, though, and as the cognitive dissonance built up, it became increasingly hard for Americans to pretend that all the atrocities and abuses of the Cold War era belonged to the other side.

Those pressures reached critical mass in the early 1970s. The Pentagon's epic incompetence in the Vietnam war and the blatant illegality and corruption of the Nixon administration sparked a backlash that, for once, reached right up into the corridors of power. In the wake of the resulting explosions, American troops came home from Southeast Asia, Nixon was forced out of office, and a quarter century of dubious and often illegal policies unexpectedly saw the light of day. All this took place during the runup to the US bicentennial, and the contrast between admittedly idealized notions of the 1770s and the awkward realities of the 1970s forced many Americans to notice the gap between what they had become and what they claimed to be.

These cultural shifts also happened, of course, as America's own oilfields reached their all-time peak production, and the coming of America's own encounter with peak oil threw a generation of easy assumptions of perpetual national prosperity into question. There were still plenty of people alive who vividly recalled the Great Depression and the austerity of the war years, and thus could get their minds around the concept that the postwar boom might be a temporary and self-canceling event, or even a corner into which the United States had backed itself. Many Americans, across a wide range of social and political positions, embraced the possibility that a prudent regard for the limits of nonrenewable resources might be a valid approach to economic and political questions, and that resource conservation and a shift toward less extravagant ways of living might be the best available options over the long term. An even broader spectrum of Americans came to believe, at least for a time, that something crucial to their nation's meaning and value had gotten lost in the rush to global empire, but might still be recovered in time to matter.

It's popular nowadays to forget that this happened, or to insist with varying degrees of cynicism that the moment of awareness couldn't have lasted. Maybe that's so, but I wonder how much of that comes from the same uneasy conscience that drives so much of today's fashionable nihilism. Americans came together during the long ordeal that began with the stock market crash of 1929 and wound its way through the shadows of depression and war until 1945, and a similar effort over a similar time scale would have been more than adequate to the task of launching America into the transition to an ecotechnic future. Back then, the US still had abundant coal, oil, and natural gas reserves, not to mention a great many other resources; annual consumption of energy and resources was far below what it later became, and though a great many factories were shuttered in the sharp recessions of the 1970s, there were still millions of capable laborers who could have been put to work retooling the economy for a new and frugal age.

The steps necessary to make that transition were discussed during that time in any number of periodicals, some of them surprisingly mainstream. The United States would have had to step back from its self-appointed role as global policeman; it would have had to pass on a fair share of the cost of deterring the Soviet Union to its comparatively more prosperous allies in western Europe and the west Pacific, and accept a less expansive notion of its own national interests. Government subsidies for nuclear power and other nonrenewable energy sources would have been phased out, and the money—along with savings from a less gargantuan military—shifted into grants for conservation, renewable energy retrofits, and research programs aimed at repositioning American industry to lead the world in green energy technologies.

Changes in tax policy, zoning regulations and building codes would reshape the built environment to decrease energy use, while funds formerly wasted on highways would go instead to build high-speed rail between urban cores and rapid transit systems that would make commuting by car all but obsolete. All this would have cost plenty, and would have required Americans to tighten their belts and accept a diminished standard of living and some formal or informal rationing for a time. Down the road a quarter century or so, though, a prosperous nation getting by comfortably on a fraction of its previous energy needs, and thus able to ignore the Middle East as an irrelevance, would have the lion's share of global trade in new energy technologies, high-speed rail, and a dozen other fields, while other nations burdened with high energy costs were left scrambling to catch up.

That was the vision. Again, it's comforting to the collective conscience of today's America to insist that it couldn't have happened, but "comforting" is rarely a synonyn for "true." Myself, I think that it could have been done, or that there was at least a very real chance of doing it. The uncomfortable silence that falls whenever anyone brings up the subject of conservation in most circles in America today is one of the reasons I've come to that belief. When people set aside an obvious impossibility, they don't remain brittle and angry about it for decades afterwards. It's only when the road not taken was a real option, and the goal at the end of it noticeably better than the endpoint looming up ahead, that those who chose otherwise get shrill in defense of their decision.

That shrill tone is hard to miss these days, and it's grown in volume and intensity over the course of the thirty-year vacation from reality America took in the aftermath of the Seventies. We'll talk more about that in next week's post.

Part Two: Lead Us Away From Here

An irony I've had the chance to relish repeatedly, over the five years or so since *The Archdruid Report* first ventured onto the blogosphere, is the extraordinary grip of convention and conformity on exactly those sectors of American society that take the most pride in their rejection of convention and conformity. It's reminiscent of the scene from the Monty Python film *Life of Brian* in which a crowd of adoring followers, told that they are all individuals, chants back in perfect unison, "Yes, we are all individuals!"

It's easy enough to laugh, but there's much to be learned from the beliefs that are taken for granted by those who insist they take nothing for granted. The subject of today's post is one of those, one that's deeply entangled with the cult of nihilism I dissected in last week's essay. It's a credo that's embraced with equal enthusiasm straight across the political spectrum from left to right, and from the middle of the road out as far toward the fringes as you care to look.

There are few better examples of groupthink in contemporary American life, and yet nearly all the people who accept the notions I have in mind are convinced that they're rebelling against conformity by conforming to a belief system shared by nearly everybody else in the country.

The credo in question? It's the belief that all the decisions that really matter in the United States today are made by a small elite, insulated from the democratic process, who are pursuing policies that would be rejected by the American people if the latter had the chance to make up their own minds.

Those of my readers who happen to be Democrats may find it educational to sit down sometime with a stalwart Republican, perhaps over a couple of beers, and ask whether this is the case. You can count on getting an earful about the corrupt liberal elite that pulls all the strings in this country. If any of my readers happen to be Republican, and try the same experiment in reverse, they can expect an equal and opposite earful about the corrupt corporate elite that pulls all the strings in this country. Step outside the two main parties and ask the same question, and you'll get at least thirty-one different flavors of the same claim, topped off, perhaps, by some follower of David Icke insisting that the corrupt elite that pulls all the strings is actually the cabal of evil space lizards that Ickes appears to have lifted from one too many viewings of the otherwise forgettable Eighties science fiction TV series *V*.

Nearly everyone agrees, in other words, that there's a corrupt elite pulling the strings, even though no two factions can agree on who it is and what they want. Next to nobody challenges the assumption that democracy is a charade controlled by unseen hands. Still, I'm convinced that it's high time to question that assumption, and to trace out its links to the cult of nihilism and the profoundly troubled national conscience that have exercised a corrosive influence on this country since the end of the Seventies.

It's probably necessary to say right off that challenging the credo

I've outlined here does not require believing in the fairy tale version of democracy too many schools still insist on dishing up to our children, in an apparent attempt to apply Huckleberry Finn's famous definition of faith—"believing what you know ain't so"—to the political sphere. In the real world, a democratic society is not a Utopia that guarantees everyone perfect liberty and equality. Rather, it's simply one way of managing the chore of making collective decisions, in the context of a society that—like all human societies everywhere—distributes wealth, power, rights, and responsibilities unequally among its citizens. I tend to think that democracy deserves our support because, by and large, it produces fewer and less drastic human rights violations and allows somewhat more individual freedom than the alternatives, but those are relative distinctions, not absolutes, and democracy also has a bumper crop of problems of its own that are hardwired into its basic architecture.

For instance, democracies always have severe problems with corruption, because democracy is one of the few systems of government in which the rich aren't automatically the ones who make collective decisions. In a hereditary aristocracy, say, the people who have the political authority also have most of the national wealth, and thus can afford the disdain for the merely rich that aristocrats so often affect. In a democracy, by contrast, there are always people who have wealth but want influence, and people who have power but want money, and the law of supply and demand takes it from there. Those who claim that the existence of political corruption in America shows that it's no longer a democracy thus have the matter exactly backwards; it's precisely because American national, state and local governments are more or less democratic that corruption flourishes here, as it has in nearly every other democracy on record.

There are plenty of other problems endemic to democracies. A glance over the ancient Greek literature on the subject, just for starters, will provide any of my readers who are curious about this with an uncomfortably exact autopsy of the current problems of American politics. Still, the most important problem with democracy is one that's inseparable from the basic idea of handing decision-making over to the citizens as a whole, because no law of nature requires a majority to be right.

Now it's central to most versions of the credo of elite rule I mentioned earlier in this post to claim that the majority is so thoroughly manipulated by the corrupt (insert partisan label here) elite pulling all the strings in this country that it can't make up its own mind about anything that matters, and simply follows the lead of the elite. Democrats, Republicans, believers in evil space lizards, and nearly everyone else pass easily from this claim to the insistence that if the majority was able to think for itself, it would back the Democrats, Republicans, believers in evil space lizards, or whoever else happens to be speaking at the time. This may in itself suggest one of the motives for this very comforting notion, but there may be more going on here than simple sour grapes.

There is, to be sure, plenty of manipulation of the public in America, as in any other democracy, for reasons identical to those behind the prevalence of corruption in democratic systems. At any given time, there may be a couple of dozen organized groups or more trying to push some set of ideas on the public by fair means or foul. What is not often recognized is that the public is not merely a passive participant in this process. Multimillion-dollar marketing campaigns routinely flop because the American public, motivated by its habitual perversity, shrugs and walks away from the most carefully crafted marketing pitch to embrace some fad or fashion nobody on Madison Avenue saw coming. That is to say, manipulation works in both directions; those people who try to bend public opinion to their own ends can succeed only by telling the public what it wants to hear.

The same thing is equally true in politics, as a glance over the history of the last half dozen decades of American political life will show clearly enough. Perhaps the best example of all is the abandonment of the movement toward sustainability in the wake of the Seventies.

That movement was backed by a loose coalition with diverse and often conflicting goals, and it faced strident opposition from a large sector of the public, but it had the support of government officials who were worried about the price of dependence on Middle Eastern oil, and who also felt the perennial need of politicians to appear to be doing something about the crisis du jour, which at that point was the high cost of energy. Some members of both parties opposed the movement, though others on both sides of the aisle backed it; some corporate interests opposed it, while others recognized that alternative energy just might turn out to be the next big thing. The entire movement, however, was based all along on the gamble that the American public would be willing to tighten its belt and plunge into the transition to an ecotechnic society even when the bills started coming due in earnest.

On the other side of the game was a coterie of Republican politicians and strategists who guessed that when push came to shove, the American public would crumple. When a chapter of accidents put their candidate into the White House, they bet the future of their party on that guess, and won. The election that mattered here wasn't Reagan's relatively narrow victory in 1980, but his landslide in 1984, when most of the nation registered its approval of a policy shift that spared them the costs of the transition to sustainability. It was after the latter election that the axe came down on funding for appropriate tech, and Woodsy Owl's iconic "Give a hoot—don't pollute!" ads vanished from the airwaves.

Notice also what happened as the Eighties unfolded. It wasn't just the American public that crumpled; the sustainability movement did, too. There were some who stayed the course, who saw that the plunge in energy prices bought by breakneck pumping of the North Slope and North Sea oil fields would turn out to be one of history's classic short-term fixes, and kept the green flame lit. Still, by and large, most of the people who had been subscribers to *Rain* and *Coevolution Quarterly*, and had been nervously trying to work up the courage to accept the restricted lifestyles they knew would be required, talked themselves into believing that the time for that was over. Several commenters on last week's post have recalled the guilty relief with which they, and so many other people, welcomed the end of gas lines and the return of cheap gasoline; it was a common sentiment at the time.

The price for that failure, though, was not limited to the collapse of a movement that might just have gotten us through the end of the petroleum age without a long and bitter age of contraction. The payoff the Reagan administration offered the American people was the same unearned prosperity that wrecks most democracies in the end. That payoff was cashed in, in turn, by cultivating a degree of fiscal irresponsibility no previous American administration had ever considered: cutting taxes, increasing government payouts, and simply borrowing the difference.

When the aftershocks of the dizzying 1987 stock market crash made the first Bush administration veer slightly in the direction of fiscal prudence, in turn, the mild economic contraction that followed was more than enough to allow Clinton to breeze to victory in 1992 with a platform that amounted to very little more than "I'll make you richer than he will." That's been the model of American politics ever since; it's not accidental that the Republican and Democratic plans to "decrease the deficit" under discussion at this moment both involve big increases in government spending, because bribing the electorate and inflating financial bubbles for their benefit are essential to get or keep office these days.

It's in this light that the behavior of the two main American political parties over the last thirty years needs to be understood. Since 1984, the Democrats' strategy has been to denounce the Republicans during each presidential campaign and then, once in office, copy GOP policies letter for letter, with the occasional sop thrown to their erstwhile allies now and then for form's sake. The hangdog, foot-scuffing spinelessness displayed repeatedly by Democratic politicians in the face of Republican pressure, I've come to believe, has its roots here; it's hard to stand firm against the opposition if you're covertly imitating all its policies.

The Republicans, for their part, have traveled an even longer road from their roots than the Democrats. Fifty years ago, the GOP was the party of small government, fiscal prudence, local autonomy, and a healthy distrust of foreign military adventures. For that matter, from the founding of the National Parks by Theodore Roosevelt to the sweeping environmental reforms enacted by Nixon, the GOP had at least as good a record on environmental issues as the Democrats. Had a delegate to a 1960 GOP county convention proposed today's Republican policies, in other words, he would have been thrown out of the hall with enough force to leave a faceprint on the pavement. The near-total betrayal of its historic commitments and ideals by today's GOP has left deep scars; I suspect that the shrill fury with which so many Republican spokespeople denounce everyone else comes from the deep and unadmitted discomfort they feel at that betrayal, and their own complicity in it.

Finally, the behavior of the Bush and Obama administrations in the wake of the 2008 crash needs to be understood in a very different sense than it's usually given. Much of the economic history of the last thirty years has been driven by the need for the political establishment to keep giving the American public what it demanded, even when those demands could only be met by a series of increasingly risky high-stakes gambles and dubiously legal expedients. The borrow-and-spend Republicans of the Reagan years relied on the ability of global capital markets to absorb an endless supply of US Treasury debt, but the imbalances set in motion by that decision forced each administration deeper into market manipulations than the last.

The huge financial corporations that played so central a role in the housing bubble, and are equally central to the current attempt to inflate a new bubble, are by all accounts key players in these schemes. Certainly there's plenty of corruption involved—again, that's endemic to democracy—and huge and arguably dishonest fortunes are being made, but there's also the hard fact that the big banks have become crucial organs of US economic policy and will be propped up by any means necessary as long as their usefulness remains. That policy has many goals, to be sure, but maintaining the facade of American prosperity demanded by the electorate, long after every real basis for that prosperity has evaporated, ranks well up among them.

Does all this mean that the electorate is uniquely responsible for what happened in the wake of the Seventies? It's hard to think of any sense in which that notion could have meaning. An entire nation made a disastrous wrong turn at that time; millions of people, each in his or her own way, contributed to that wrong turn, and very, very few opposed it. At this stage in the game, trying to affix blame to any narrower subset of the nation may be popular but it's also useless, as it simply feeds the nihilism this series of posts is anatomizing. Clinging to the fashionable belief in the omnipotence of evil elites is the extreme form of that blame game, and even more useless than most of the others. The hard but necessary task before us, instead, is to come to terms with the fact that our nation made a catastrophic mistake thirty years ago, and that most of us who were alive at that time either backed that mistake or acquiesced in it.

Ironically enough, given that this series of posts started with a reference to a bit of Seventies popular music, it was another Seventies band—Styx, in the closing lines of the 1975 hit "Suite Madam Blue"—that did as good a job as anyone of stating the challenge we as a nation faced at the close of that decade, calling America to "make a new start" and "lead us away from here." We failed that challenge then. In the final part of this series of posts, we'll talk about the options for meeting it now.

Part Three: A Horse With No Name

A bit of retrospective may be useful at this point, as we close in on the core of the argument I've been developing here. The first post in this series, "A Dog Named Boo," explored the sudden turn toward nihilism that seized America's culture and public imagination in the wake of the Seventies; the second, "Lead Us Away From Here," analyzed the fantasy of elite omnipotence and public powerlessness that became conventional wisdom straight across the political spectrum in the wake of that shift.

The connection between the shift and the fantasy may not be instantly obvious to all my readers, but it can be made a good deal clearer by looking more closely at what happened as the Seventies ended and our society's thirty-year vacation from reality began. During the Seventies, a great many Americans came face to face with the hard fact that they could have the comfortable and privileged lifestyles they were used to having, or they could guarantee a livable world for their grandchildren, but they couldn't do both. The vast majority of them—or, more precisely, of us— chose the first option and closed their eyes to the consequences. That mistake was made for understandable and profoundly human reasons, but it was still a mistake, and it haunts the American imagination to this day.

The impact of that choice is perhaps easier to trace on the conservative end of America's social and political spectrum. Forty years ago, the Republicans had at least as good a record on environmental issues as the Democrats, and the idolatry of the unrestrained free market that pervades the American right these days was a fringe ideology widely, and rightly, considered suspect by most conservatives. For that matter, creationism and speculations about the imminence of the End Times were consigned to the fringes

62

by most American Christians, who by and large considered them irrelevant to the task of living a life centered on the teachings of the Christian gospel.

All these things changed in a hurry at the end of the Seventies. Why? Because the attitudes that replaced them—the shrill insistence that the environment doesn't matter, that the free market will solve every problem, that the world was created in 4004 BCE with as much oil, coal, and gas as God wants us to have, and that the world will end in our lifetimes so our grandchildren won't have to deal with the mess we'd otherwise be leaving them—are all attempts to brush aside the ugly fact that the choices made at the end of the Seventies, and repeated by most Americans at every decision point since then, have cashed in the chance of a better future for our grandchildren, and spent the proceeds on an orgy of consumption in the present.

The squirmings of the leftward end of American culture and politics are a little subtler, since the Left by and large responded to the end of the Seventies by clinging to its historic ideals, while quietly shelving any real attempt to do anything about them. It's discomfort with this response that leads so many people on the Left to insist angrily that they've done all they can reasonably be expected to do about the environment, in the midst of pursuing a lifestyle that's difficult to distinguish, on any basis but that of sheer fashion, from that of their Republican neighbors. It also drives the frankly delusional insistence on the part of so many people on today's Left that everyone on Earth can aspire to a middle class American lifestyle if the evil elites already discussed would simply let it happen, and the equally, if more subtly, delusional claim that some suite of technologies currently in the vaporware stage will permit the American middle class to have its planet and eat it too.

Look beyond the realm of partisan quarrels and the same deeply troubled conscience appears over and over again in American life. Consider, as one example out of many, the way that protecting children turned from a reasonable human concern to an obsessive-compulsive fixation. Raised under the frantic surveillance of helicopter moms, forbidden from playing outside or even visiting another child's home except on the basis of a prearranged and parentally approved play date, a generation of American children were held hostage by a galaxy of parental terrors that have only the most distorted relationship to reality, but serve to distract attention from the fact that the lifestyles chosen by these same parents were condemning their children to a troubled and dangerous life in a depleted, polluted, and impoverished world.

The irony reached a dizzying intensity as tens of thousands of American parents rushed out to buy SUVs to transport their children to places every previous generation of American children proved perfectly capable of reaching by themselves on foot or on bike. It became the conventional wisdom, during the peak of the SUV craze, that the safety provided to young passengers by these massive rolling fortresses justified their purchase. No one wanted to deal with the fact that it was precisely the lifestyle exemplified by the SUV that was, and remains, the single most pressing threat to children's long-term safety and welfare.

A great many of the flailings and posturings that have defined American culture from the Eighties to the present, in other words, unfolded from what Jean-Paul Sartre called "bad faith"—the unspoken awareness, however frantically denied or repressed, that the things that actually mattered were not things anyone was willing to talk about, and that the solutions everyone wanted to discuss were not actually aimed at their putative targets. The lie at the heart of that bad faith was the desperate attempt to avoid facing the implications of the plain and utterly unwelcome fact that there is no way to make a middle class American lifestyle sustainable.

Let's repeat that, just for the sake of emphasis: *there is no way to make a middle class American lifestyle sustainable.*

That's the elephant in the living room, the thing that most of a nation has been trying not to see, and not to say, for so many years. The middle class American lifestyle, to borrow and extend Jim Kunstler's useful decription of suburbia,[*] is an arrangement without a future. It's utterly dependent on the rapid exploitation of irreplaceable resources, and the longer that it's pursued, and the more people pursue it, the worse the consequences will be for children now living, and for a great many generations not yet born. It really is as simple as that.

Now it's not at all hard to find books, films, websites, and speakers who say as much, but it's intriguing to watch how universally these avoid the next logical step. What do you do if you're pursuing a way of life that has no future? Well, apparently you read books denouncing that way of life, or heap praise on cultures conveniently distant in space or time that you think had or have or will have a different way of life, or engage in token activities intended to show that your heart really isn't in that way of life, or vent your rage against whoever it is that you blame for your decision to keep on following that way of life, or fixate with increasing desperation on manufactured prophecies insisting that the Rapture or the Singularity or the space brothers or somebody, anybody, will bring that way of life to an end for you so that you don't have to do it yourself.

The one thing you apparently don't do is the one thing that actually matters, which is changing the way you live here and now.

That's the rock on which the sustainability movement of the Seventies broke, and it's claimed plenty of victims since then. The climate change movement is a good recent example. Now it's true that there were plenty of reasons why the climate change movement followed the trajectory it did from apparent unstoppability a decade ago to its current dead-in-the-water status today. The ingenuousness with which climate change activists allowed their opponents to

---

[*] see specially James Howard Kunstler, *The Geography of Nowhere* (New York: Free Press, 1993)

redefine the terms of the debate very nearly at will, and the movement's repeated attempts to rest its arguments on the faltering prestige of science in an age when most Americans are well aware that scientific opinions can be purchased to order for the cost of a modest grant, did not help the cause any.

Still, I've come to think that the Achilles' heel of the entire movement was the simple fact that none of its spokespersons showed any willingness to embrace the low-energy lifestyle they insisted the rest of the world had to adopt. Al Gore, with his sprawling air-conditioned mansion and his frequent jet trips, was the poster child here, but he had plenty of company. It was because climate change activists so often failed to walk their talk, I suggest, that millions of Americans decided they must be making the whole thing up, just as the obvious eagerness of the United States to push carbon limits on every other nation while refusing to accept them at home convinced China among others that the global warming crusade was simply one more gimmick to prop up the crumbling edifice of American hegemony, and brought the movement toward a worldwide carbon treaty to the standstill where it remains today.

The same blind spot continues to plague what's left of the climate change movement. Consider former environmentalist Stewart Brand, who used to edit *The Whole Earth Catalog*, for heaven's sake. Brand's current position, retailed at length in his recent book *Whole Earth Discipline*, is that we have to run our economy on nuclear power because burning coal is bad for the environment. Now of course this argument is right up there with insisting that shooting yourself through the head is good for your health because it prevents you from dying of a heart attack, but there's a deeper irrationality here. Ironically, it's one that most people who had copies of *The Whole Earth Catalog* on their shelves forty years ago could have pointed out in a Sausalito minute: switching from one complex, centralized, environmentally destructive energy system based on nonrenewable and rapidly depleting resources, to another energy system that can be described in exactly the same terms, is not a useful step—especially when it would be perfectly possible to dispense with both by simply using less energy.

Now of course the concept of using less of anything is about as popular in contemporary America as garlic aioli at a convention of vampires. Nobody wants to be reminded that using less, so that our grandchildren would have enough, was the road we didn't take at the end of the Seventies. Still, the road we did take was always destined to be a dead end, and as we move deeper into the first half of the twenty-first century, the end of that road is starting to come into sight. At this point, we're faced with the prospect of using less energy, not because we choose to do so but because the energy that would be needed to do otherwise isn't there any more. That's the problem with living as though there's no tomorrow, of course: tomorrow inevitably shows up anyway.

This late in the game, our remaining options are starkly limited, and most of the proposals you'll hear these days are simply variations on the theme of chasing business as usual right over the nearest cliff. Whether it's Stewart Brand's nukes, "Drill Baby Drill," ethanol or algal biodiesel or some other kind of energy vaporware, the subtext to every widely touted response to our predicament is that we don't need to use less. The same thing's just as true of most of the ideologies that claim to offer a more global response to that predicament; the one common thread that unites the neoprimitivists who claim to long for a return to the hunter-gatherer life, the conspiracy theorists who spend their days in an increasingly frantic orgy of fingerpointing, and the apocalypticists who craft ever more elaborate justifications for the claim that somebody or other will change the world for us, is that each of these ideologies, and plenty others like them, function covertly as justifications to allow believers to keep on living an ordinary American lifestyle right up to the moment that it drops away from beneath their feet.

The one option that doesn't do this is the one next to nobody is willing to talk about, and that's the option of using less.

Mention that option in public, and inevitably you'll hear a dozen different reasons why it can't help and won't matter and isn't practical anyway. Can it help? Of course it can; in a time when world crude oil production has been bouncing against a hard ceiling for most of a decade and most other energy sources are under growing strain, any decrease in the amount of energy being wasted on nonessentials makes it a little easier to keep essential services up and running. Will it matter? Of course it will; as we move into a future of hard energy constraints, the faster at least a few people get through the learning curve of conservation, appropriate tech, and simply making do with less, the easier it will be for the rest of society to follow their lead and learn from their experience, if only when all the other choices have been foreclosed. Is it practical? Of course it is; the average European gets by comfortably on one third the annual energy budget as the average American, and it's been my experience that most middle class Americans can slash their energy use by a third or more in one year by a relatively simple program of home weatherizing and lifestyle changes.

I'd like to suggest, in fact, that at this point in the trajectory of industrial civilization, any proposal that doesn't make using less energy a central strategy simply isn't serious. It's hard to think of any dimension of our predicament that can't be bettered, often dramatically, by using less energy, and even harder to think of any project that will yield significant gains as long as Americans cling to a lifestyle that history is about to relegate to the compost bin. I'd also like to suggest that any proposal that does start out with using less energy should not be taken seriously until and unless the people proposing it actually do use less energy themselves, preferably by adopting the measures they urge on others.

That's how effective movements for social change happen, after all. Individuals start them by making changes in their own lives; as the number of people making those changes grows, networks emerge to share information, resources, and encouragement; the networks become the frame of a subculture, and as momentum builds, the subculture becomes a movement. It's indicative that the two movements that had the most impact on American culture in the second half of the twentieth century—feminism and Christian fundamentalism—both emerged this way, starting with individuals who changed their own lives, while any number of movements that tried to make change from the top down—again, the climate change movement is a good example—failed to achieve their ends.

That's the core concept behind the "green wizardry"[*] I've been discussing here on *The Archdruid Report* for almost a year now. It's entirely possible for each of us to kick the process just described into motion by using less energy and fewer natural resources in our own lives. There are proven methods and mature technologies that will accomplish that. It so happens that I learned some of those back in the early 1980s, and have a couple of decades of experience applying them in my own life. That's been the basis on which I've selected the tools and techniques discussed here; for reasons already explained, I don't think it's useful to advocate things I haven't used myself.

The one great barrier in the path of starting a movement the right way, beginning on the individual level, is that it requires each person who takes up the challenge to break with the conventional wisdom and do things that others aren't prepared to do. That's a lonely journey, no question, and since this series of posts began with a bit of Seventies music, I don't think it's out of place to end it with a reference to the most famous desert journey from the music of that era, America's "Horse With No Name." To borrow a turn of phrase from the song, that loneliness can be a place to remember our names or, more precisely, to recall that we have names other than "consumer" and "victim."

It's my hope that at least some of the people who read this post

---

[*] Those posts became the core of my book *Green Wizardry*.

will rise to that challenge. We've got a lot of work to do, and there may not be much time to get it started before conditions become a good deal more difficult than they are right now. I'll be discussing that last point in more detail in the weeks ahead.

Salvaging Learning

(Originally published 27 July 2011)

The other day, courtesy of the public library system here in Cumberland, I had the chance to curl up on the couch with a copy of Canadian journalist Jonathan Kay's survey of American conspiracy theorists, *Among the Truthers*. I'm sorry to say it was a disappointing read. Kay's an engaging writer and the book has some good moments, but on the whole it was a depressing reminder of the reasons that the word "journalistic" has become a synonym for "facile and tendentious."

This is doubly unfortunate, because the issues Kay was trying to raise are worth discussing. Over the last couple of decades, ordinary political discourse in America has been drowned out by a torrent of hatred and rage—there is really no other way to describe it—directed by people on nearly every part of the political spectrum against their perceived opponents. These days it's become a commonplace of American political culture to insist that the world's problems result from the deliberate malevolence of some group of people or other, whose intentions and historical role are portrayed with a degree of moral extremism that would make a third-century Gnostic gulp in disbelief. How many times, dear reader, have you seen blog posts and newspaper articles—we don't even need to bring in the gutterslop that sloshes through talk radio these days—that flatten out the complex ambiguities of industrial civilization's spiralling crises into an insistence that somebody or other is wrecking the world out of pure personal wickedness? This is the sort of thing I mean.

The bipartisan rise of this sort of hate politics in America, in turn, provides an exact parallel to the rise of the conspiracy theory movement that Kay tried to examine. Insist that George W. Bush was the puppet of a cabal of fascists plotting to conquer the world, or that Barack Obama is a socialist out to reduce Americans to slavery under a global dictatorship, and then it's hardly a leap to go on to argue that Bush's handlers masterminded the 9/11 attacks or that Obama is a Muslim illegal immigrant with a forged birth certificate. Argue for either of these latter, in turn, and you can use it to bolster your case for the limitless wickedness of your *bête du jour*.

It would take a book considerably more substantial than Kay's to sort out the tangled roots of this twin pandemic of hatred and paranoia. For the moment, I want to focus on just one of the many factors involved, both because it's not usually discussed in this context and because it's deeply relevant to the project of this blog.

Every June, across America, a couple of million high school seniors go through graduation ceremonies in our nation's public schools and receive the diploma that, once upon a time, certified that they had completed the general course of education proper to the citizen of a democracy. Nowadays, a sizable fraction of those graduates are functionally illiterate. More than half of them have no real notion how their government works and what the rest of the world is like, and have never had more than a passing glimpse of the major works of art, literature, and music that define America's cultural heritage. All but a tiny fraction of them have never learned how to reason from premises to a conclusion or check the credentials of a fact.

I'm not at all sure how many of my readers outside the United States have any idea just how bad the state of education has gotten here. A pervasive philosophy of education that reduces its role to that of job training, cultural squabbles that have stripped curriculums of most of their meaningful content, reforms that made the careers of teachers and the finances of districts depend on standardized test scores and thus guaranteed that teaching students how to score high on those tests would be given priority over everything else, budget cuts that always get taken out of classroom expenses rather than administrative costs—well, you can do the math yourself. There are exceptions, but on the whole the public schools in America do a miserably poor job of teaching anything but contempt for learning.

Higher education is a more complex situation but, in some ways, an even more toxic one. Where the public schools trudge implacably onwards under the iron law of bureaucracy, colleges and universities have become an industry, governed by ethics no better than any other American business. It's possible to get a good education from an American university if you're lucky, smart, and ruthless, but there are significant obstacles you'll have to get past. The most important are, first, that the university system is more or less designed to leave you a quarter million dollars or so in debt by the time you finish your degree program, without the option of bankruptcy—college loans are federally guaranteed, meaning that the courts can't discharge them—and, second, while the academic industry presents itself as a ticket to high-paying careers, the great majority of college degree programs don't do anything of the kind. It's been shown repeatedly that the vast majority of high school seniors who enter university now will never recover financially from the economic burden of paying off their student loans.

No doubt a case could be made, and no doubt it will be made, that the exposure to learning that comes from a college education is worth a lifetime of financial impoverishment. The difficulty with such claims is that the philosophy of education as job training that helped gut America's public schools has done much the same thing to higher education, even in fields—such as the humanities—that sometimes claim to be exempt from the trend. In most of today's American universities, despite a certain amount of lip service, humanities programs no longer fulfill their historic role of giving students a broad introduction to humanity's cultural and intellectual heritage. Their focus instead is on the job training needed by future professors in one or another narrow subspecialty. Departments have to justify their existence in today's academic industry by maximizing enrollment, however, and this means that degree programs in the humanities not only admit, but actively recruit, far more students every year than are needed to meet the demand for new professors of film studies, postcolonial literature, comparative history of ideas, and the like. That's the reason why, as the joke goes, the first thing a liberal arts major says when he or she goes to work after graduation is "Would you like fries with that?"

Now factor in the multiple economic impacts of peak oil on a sprawling, dysfunctional collection of government bureacracies, on the one hand, and a corrupt and rapacious industry totally dependent on abundant credit and government loan guarantees, on the other. At the least, it's a recipe for the end of American education as it's currently practiced, and it's not implausible that unless something else gets patched together in a hurry, it could mean the end of American education, period.

Like the rest of America's bureaucracies and industries, education in this country got onto its current trajectory of metastatic growth in the aftermath of the Second World War, when oceans of cheap fossil fuel energy and the considerable benefits of global hegemony made no price tag look too big. When the wave of homegrown fossil fuel crested in the early 1970s, in turn, Americans—who even then were willing to blame almost anything for their troubles, other than the irritating unwillingness of the laws of physics to give them a limitless supply of energy—decided to double down and bluff, for all the world as though acting out the fantasy that we'd have plenty of energy and resources in the future would force the bluff to turn into reality.

The realization most Americans are frantically trying to stave off just now is that nature has called our bluff. That limitless new supply of energy most of us were waiting for hasn't appeared, and there are good reasons, founded in the laws of physics, to think that it never will. In the meantime, our decision to double down has left us burdened with, among other things, a public school system and a collection of colleges and universities even more gargantuan and unaffordable than the ones we had before we doubled down, and a psychology of previous investment that all but guarantees that our society will keep on throwing good money after bad until there's nothing left to throw. Politicians and ordinary people alike have taken to insisting, along these lines, that the solution to joblessness is to send people to college to get job training, on the assumption that this will somehow make jobs appear for them. To call this magical thinking is an insult to honest sorcerers, but it's likely to be increasingly common in the years to come—at least until the bottom drops out completely.

Well before that happens, a system that's already largely irrelevant to the needs of the present shows every sign of making itself completely irrelevant to the even more pressing challenges of the future. If anything is going to be salvaged from the wreckage, it's going to have to be done by individuals who commit themselves to the task on their own time. To make sense of such a project, though, it's going to be necessary to face a far more basic question: what, exactly, is the point of education?

That's a far more complex question than it seems, because American culture has spent the last few decades at the far end of a pendulum swing between two sharply different understandings of education—and indeed of human knowledge itself. Call them abstraction and reflection. Abstraction is the view that holds that behind the hubbub and confusion of everyday life lies a fundamental order that can be known by the human mind, and accurately expressed by means of abstract generalizations—$E=MC^2$, the law of supply and demand, the theory of evolution, or what have you. In an age dominated by abstraction, knowledge tends to be equated with these abstract generalizations, and education becomes a matter of teaching students to memorize them, apply them, and maybe add to the sum total of known generalizations.

Abstraction tends to predominate when civilizations are expanding. It's a confident viewpoint, both in its faith that the human mind is capable of knowing the inner workings of the cosmos, and in its claims that its method for generating abstractions is applicable to all subjects and that its particular set of abstract generalizations equate to objective truth. Of course the faith and the claims run into trouble sooner or later; whatever method the civilization uses to determine truth—classical logic in ancient Greece, Christian theology in medieval Europe, experimental science in modern America—eventually ends up in paradox and self-contradiction, and the irreducible cussedness of nature turns the first elegant generalizations into clanking, overburdened theoretical machinery that eventually falls apart of its own weight. Meanwhile Utopian hopes of a society of reason and enlightenment, which partisans of abstraction always seem to cherish, run headlong into the hard realities of human nature: after Athens' golden age, the Peloponnesian War and the self-destruction of Greek democracy; after the Gothic cathedrals and the great medieval summae, the Black Death and the Hundred Years War; after the brilliant trajectory of science from Galileo to Einstein—well, we'll be around to see the opening stages of that.

That's when reflection comes into play. Reflection is the view that recognizes that human ideas of the order of the cosmos are, in the final analysis, just another set of human ideas, and that the hubbub and confusion of everyday life is the only reality we can be sure of. In an age dominated by reflection, Giambattista Vico's great maxim—"we can truly know only what we make"—takes center stage, and humanity rather than the cosmos becomes the core object of knowledge. It's not a knowledge that can be extracted in the form of abstract generalizations, either; it's a personal, tacit knowledge, a knowledge woven of examples, intuitions, and things felt rather than things defined. From the standpoint of abstraction, of course, this isn't knowledge at all, but in practical application it works surprisingly well; a sensitivity to circumstances and a memory well stocked with good examples and concrete maxims tend, if anything, to be more useful in the real world than an uncritical reliance on the constructions of current theory.

This is why Greek intellectual culture, with its focus on logic, mathematics, physics, and speculative philosophy, gave way to Roman intellectual culture, which focused instead on literature, history, jurisprudence, and ethical philosophy. It's also why the culture of the high Middle Ages, with its soaring ambition to understand the cosmos by interpreting religious revelation in the light of reason, gave way to the *humaniores litterae*—literally, the more human writings—of the Renaissance, which focused attention back on humanity, not as an object under the not-yet-invented microscope, but as a subject capable of knowing and acting in a complex, unpredictable world. It's by way of reference to those "more human writings" that we still call the characteristic interests of Renaissance culture "the humanities."

Next week's post will follow the most recent swing of the pendulum over to the side of abstraction, since that has to be understood in order to sort out what can be saved from contemporary science. Here, though, I want to spare a few moments for the almost completely neglected issue of the value of the humanities in an age of collapse. Modern American culture is so deeply invested in abstraction that the very suggestion that reflection, as I've defined it, could have pragmatic value as a way of knowledge seems ludicrous to most people. Still, given that we've landed ourselves in the usual trap that comes with overcommitment to abstraction—we can determine beyond a shadow of a doubt what has to be done, and prove that it has to be done, but we've become completely incapable of motivating people to do it—a strong case could be made that we need to pay more attention to that aspect of knowledge and culture that deals directly with human existence in its actual context of complexity and rootedness, an aspect that offers no general laws but many practical insights.

There's another reason why it may be worthwhile to refocus on reflection rather than abstraction in the years ahead of us. As already mentioned, the partisans of abstraction have a hard time finding any value at all in reflection; Plato's insistence that poets ought to be chucked out the gates of his Republic, John Scotus Erigena's dismissal of core elements of the humanities because "they do not appear to have to do with the nature of things," Descartes' irritable condemnation of literary studies, and the fulminations of today's scientific pundits against any dimension of human experience that can't be measured on some kind of dial, all come from this habit of thought.

Curiously, though, the reverse is rarely the case. In ages when reflection predominates, the sciences tend to be preserved and transmitted to the future along with the humanities, because the sciences are also products of human thought and culture; they can be studied as much for what they reveal about humanity as for what they reveal about nature. That shift has already been taking place; when the late Carl Sagan spun his compelling "We are star-stuff" myth for the viewers of *Cosmos*, for example, he was engaging in reflection rather than abstraction. Hs goal was not to communicate an abstract rule but to weave a narrative of meaning that provided a context within which human life can be lived.

The modern American educational system is by and large the last place on earth to try to pursue or communicate any such vision, whether undergirded by Saganism or some more traditionally religious standpoint. Equally, though, as I've already pointed out, the modern American educational system is very poorly positioned indeed to deal with the impacts of peak oil, and the rest of the smorgasbord of crises the bad decisions of the last few decades have set out for us. The question that remains is what might replace it. What will come after the public schools is already taking shape, in the form of a lively and successful homeschooling movement that routinely turns out the sort of educated young people public schools once did; the replacement for what's left of America's once thriving trade schools is less well organized and defined as yet, but is emerging as craftspeople take on apprentices and people interested in a dizzying array of crafts form networks of mutual support. What we don't yet have is a replacement for what the universities used to offer—some form of organized activity, however decentralized, informal, and inexpensive, that will see to the preservation and transmission of the intellectual heritage of our age.

What form such a thing might take is a challenging question, and one for which I don't have any immediate answers. Still, it's an issue that needs to be addressed. The pervasive spread of paranoiac conspiracy theories in contemporary American culture, which I mentioned toward the beginning of this post, is only one of several signs that too many people in this country have never learned how to doublecheck the validity of their own thinking, either against the principles of logic—a core element of the cultural heritage of abstraction—or against that attentiveness to circumstances and human motives that comes from "more human writings"—a core element of the cultural heritage of reflection. The people who chant "Drill, baby, drill," as though it's an incantation that will summon barrels of oil from thin air, are doing just as poor a job of reasoning about the world and reflecting on their motivations as the people who use the unprepossessing individuals teetering on the upper end of our political class as inkblots on which to project their need for scapegoats and their fantasies of absolute evil.

Working out the first rough sketch of a replacement for the American academic industry won't stop the incantations or the scapegoating any time soon, and arguably will not stop it at all. Many other forces, as I suggested earlier, drive the contemporary flight from the muddled complexities of civil society into a comic-book world of supervillains whose alleged malignity is so clearly a product of the believer's need to find someone to blame. Yet the tasks facing those of us who are trying to get ready for the unraveling of industrial America, and the comparable tasks our grandchildren and our grandchildren's grandchildren will face, will demand plenty of clear, perceptive, well-informed thinking, guided both by abstraction's useful generalizations and by reflection's sharpened sensitivities. Doing something to salvage learning, while there's still a chance to do so, is one potentially crucial way to help that happen.

An Elegy for the
Age of Space
(Originally published 24 August 2011)

The orbiters are silent now, waiting for the last awkward journey that will take them to the museums that will warehouse the grandest of our civilization's failed dreams. There will be no countdown, no pillar of flame to punch them through the atmosphere and send them whipping around the planet at orbital speeds. All of that is over.

In Houston, the same silence creeps through rooms where technicians once huddled over computer screens as voices from space crackled over loudspeakers. The screens are black now, the mission control rooms empty, and most of the staff have already gotten their pink slips. On the Florida coast, where rusting gantries creak in the wind and bats flutter in cavernous buildings raised for the sake of a very different kind of flight, another set of lauch pads sinks slowly into their new career as postindustrial ruins.

There are still rockets lifting off elsewhere, to be sure, adding to the globe's collection of satellites and orbiting space junk. The International Space Station still wheels through the sky, visited at intervals by elderly Soyuz capsules, counting down the days and the missions until its currently scheduled deorbiting in 2016. In America, a few big corporations have manned space projects on the drawing boards, angling for whatever federal funding survives the next few rounds of our national bankruptcy proceedings, and a few billionaires here and elsewhere are building hobby spacecraft in roughly the same spirit that inspired their Gilded Age equivalents to maintain luxury yachts and thoroughbred stables.

Still, something has shifted. A tide that was expected to flow for generations and centuries to come has peaked and begun to ebb. There will still be rockets surging up from their launch pads for years or decades to come, and some few of them will have human beings on board, but the momentum is gone. It's time to start coming to terms with the winding down of the age of space.

Ironically, one of the best pieces of evidence for that was the shrill reception given to an article in *The Economist* announcing "The End of the Space Age[*]." The irony was particularly delicious in that *The Economist* is a British periodical, and Britain has already been through its own retreat from space. During the first half of the twentieth century, the British Interplanetary Society was among the most prestigious groups calling for manned space missions, but dreams of a British presence in space collapsed around the same time as Britain's empire and industrial economy did. It's hard to miss the schadenfreude in *The Economist*'s editorial stance, but it was even harder to overlook the bluster and denial splashed across the blogosphere in its wake.

A little perspective might be useful here. When the space shuttle first came off the drawing boards, the much-repeated theory was that it would be the first of a new breed of spacecraft that would make a flight from Cape Canaveral to orbit as commonplace as a flight from New York to Chicago. The next generation would swap out the shuttle's disposable fuel tank and solid-fuel boosters for a fully reusable first stage that would take a shuttle-equivalent most of the way into orbit, then come back to Earth under its own power and get refueled for the next launch. Further down the road, but already in the concept phase, were spaceplanes that could take off from an ordinary runway, use standard jet engines to get to 50,000 feet or so,

---

[*] http://www.economist.com/node/18897425

where rocket engines would cut in for the leap to orbit. Single-use rockets? In the minds of the space-savvy, they were already as outdated as Model T Fords.

Yet here we are in 2011, the space shuttle program is over, the replacements weren't built, and for the five years of scheduled life the International Space Station has left, its crews will be getting there via the 1960s-era technology of Soyuz space capsules atop single-use rockets. As for the rest of the steps toward space everyone in the 1960s assumed we would have taken by now—the permanent space stations, the base on the Moon, the manned missions to Mars, and the rest of it—only the most hardcore space fans talk about them any more, and let's not even discuss their chances of getting significant funding this side of the twelfth of never.

Mind you, I'm not cheering. Though I realized some years ago that humanity isn't going to the stars—not now, not in the lifetime of our species—the end of the shuttle program with no replacement in sight still hit me like a body blow. It's not just a generational thing, though it's partly that; another large part of it was growing up where and when I did. By that I don't just mean in the United States in the middle decades of the last century, but specifically in the triumphant years between John Glenn's first orbital flight and Neil Armstrong's final step onto lunar soil, in a suburb south of Seattle where every third family or so had a father who worked in the aerospace industry. Yes, I remember exactly where I was sitting and what was happening the moment that Walter Cronkite told the world that Apollo 11 had just landed on the Moon.

You didn't grow up as a geeky, intellectual kid in that sort of setting without falling in love with space. Of course it didn't hurt that the media was filled to the bursting point with space travel— turn on the tube any evening during my childhood, and if you didn't get *Lost In Space* or *Star Trek* you'd probably catch *The Invaders* or *My Favorite Martian*—and children's books were no different; among my favorites early on was *Ronnie Rocket and Suzie Saucer*, and I went from there to *The Wonderful Flight to the Mushroom Planet, The Spaceship Under the Apple Tree*—well, you get the picture. (I won't even get into science fiction here; that's a subject that deserves an entire post to itself.) Toys? The G.I. Joe accessory I treasured most in those days was a plastic Mercury space capsule with space suit to match; I also played with Major Matt Mason, Man In Space, and plenty of less efficiently marketed toys as well.

The future that most people imagined in those days had plenty of options primed to catch a young boy's imagination, to be sure. Sealab—does *anybody* remember Sealab these days?—was the Navy's attempt to compete with the romance of space, complete with breathless *National Geographic* articles about "a new world of limitless resources beneath the sea." (Ahem.) For a while, I followed Sealab as passionately as I did the space program, and yes, my G.I. Joe also had a wetsuit and scuba gear. That was common enough, and so were my less scientific fixations of the time, the monster lore and paranormal phenomena and the like; when you're stuck growing up in suburbia in a disintegrating family and the only source of hope you can come up with is the prospect that the world isn't as tepidly one-dimensional as everyone around you insists it has to be, you take encouragement where you find it.

You might think that a kid who was an expert on werewolf trivia at age ten would have gone in for the wildest of space fantasies, but I didn't. *Star Trek* always seemed hokey to me. (I figured out early on that *Star Trek* was a transparent pastiche of mid-1960s US foreign policy, with the Klingons as Russia, the Vulcans as Japan, the Romulans as Red China, and Captain Kirk as a wish-fulfillment fantasy version of Gen. William Westmoreland who always successfully pacified his extraterrestrial Vietnams.) Quite the contrary; my favorite spacecraft model kit, which hung from a length of thread in my bedroom for years, was called the Pilgrim Observer: some bright kit designer's vision of one of the workhorse craft of solar system exploration in the late twentieth century.

Dilithium crystals, warp drives, and similar improbabilities had no place in the Pilgrim Observer. Instead, it had big tanks for hydrogen fuel, a heavily shielded nuclear engine on a long boom aft, an engagingly clunky command module up front bristling with telescopes and dish antennas—well, here again, you get the picture; if you know your way around 1970s space nonfiction, you know the kit. It came with a little booklet outlining the Pilgrim I's initial flyby missions to Mars and Venus, all of it entirely plausible by the standards the time. That was what delighted me. Transporter beams and faster-than-light starflight, those were fantasy, but I expected to watch something not too far from Pilgrim I lifting off from Cape Canaveral within my lifetime.

That didn't happen, and it's not going to happen. That was a difficult realization for me to reach, back in the day, and it's one a great many Americans are doing their level best to avoid right now. There are two solid reasons why the future in space so many of us thought we were going to get never arrived, and each one provides its own reasons for evasion. We've talked about both of them in this blog at various times, and there's more than the obvious reason to review them now.

The first, simply put, is that the United States has lost the space race. Now of course it was less a single race than a whole track and field competition, with the first event, the satellite shot-put contest (winner: Russia, with Sputnik I), followed by the single-orbit dash (winner: Russia, with Vostok I) and a variety of longer sprints (winner: much more often than not, Russia). The run to the Moon was the first real US gold medal—we did half a dozen victory laps back out there just to celebrate—and we also scored big in the planetary probe toss competition, with a series of successful Mariner and Voyager missions that mostly showed us just how stunningly inhospitable the rest of the solar system was. The race that ultimately counted, though, was the marathon, and Russia's won that one hands down; they're still in space, and we aren't.

85

Behind that unwelcome news is the great geopolitical fact of the early 21st century, the decline and imminent fall of the American empire. Like any number of empires before us, we've gotten ourselves wedged tightly into the predictable downside of hegemony—the stage at which the costs of maintaining the economic imbalances that channel wealth from empire to imperial state outstrip the flow of wealth those imbalances are meant to produce. Once that stage arrives, the replacement of the failing empire by some new distribution of power is a foregone conclusion; the only question is how long the process will take and how brutal the final cost to the imperial state will turn out to be.

The Cold War competition between the United States and the Soviet Union was a standard contest to see which empire would outlast the other. The irony, and it's a rich one, is that the loser of that contest was pretty much guaranteed to be the winner in a broader sense. When the Soviet Union collapsed, Russia had an empire wrenched out of its hands, and as a result it was forced to give up the struggle to sustain the unsustainable. The United States kept its empire intact, and as a result it has continued that futile but obsessive fight, stripping its national economy to the bare walls in order to prop up a global military presence that will sooner or later bankrupt it completely. That's why Russia still has a functioning space program, while the United States may have trouble finding the money to launch cheap fireworks by the time its empire finally slips from its fingers.

It's our decidedly mixed luck, as discussed here more than once in the past, that America is entering on the downslope of its imperial decline just as a much vaster curve has peaked and begun to arc in the same direction. That's the second reason that the space age is ending, not just for us but for humanity. In the final analysis, space travel was simply the furthest and most characteristic offshoot of industrial civilization, and depended—as all of industrial civilization depends—on vast quantities of cheap, highly concentrated, readily accessible energy. That basic condition is coming to an end around us right now. Petroleum has already reached its global production peak as depletion rates shoot past the rate at which new fields can be found and brought on line; natural gas and coal are not far behind—the current bubble in shale gas will be over in five or, just possibly, ten years—and despite decades of animated handwaving, no other energy source has proven to yield anything close to the same abundance and concentration of energy at anything like the same cost.

That means, as I've shown in detail in past posts here, that industrial civilization will be a short-lived and self-terminating phenomenon. It doesn't mean, or at least doesn't have to mean, that future civilizations will have to make do with an equivalent of the much simpler technological suites that civilizations used before the industrial age; I've argued at some length here and elsewhere that an ecotechnic society—a civilization that supports a relatively advanced technology on a modest scale using the diffuse and limited energy provided by sustainable sources, without wrecking the planet—is a live option, if not in the immediate future, then after the dark age the misguided choices of the recent past have prepared for us.

Still, of the thousands of potential technological projects that might appeal to the limited ambitions and even more strictly limited resources of some future ecotechnic society, space travel will rank very, very low. It's possible that the thing will be done, perhaps in the same spirit that motivated China a little while back to carry out a couple of crisp, technically efficient manned orbital flights; ten thousand years from now, putting a human being into orbit will still probably be the most unanswerable way for a civilization to announce that it's arrived. There are also useful things to be gained by lofting satellites for communication and observation purposes, and it's not at all impossible that now and then, over the centuries and millennia to come, the occasional satellite will pop up into orbit for a while, and more space junk will be added to the collection already in place.

That's not the vision that fired a generation with enthusiasm for space, though. It's not the dream that made Konstantin Tsiolkovsky envision Earth as humanity's cradle, that set Robert Goddard building rockets in a Michigan farmyard and hurled Yuri Gagarin into orbit aboard Vostok I. Of all people, it was historical theorist Oswald Spengler who characterized that dream most precisely, anatomizing the central metaphor of what he called Faustian civilization—yes, that's us—as an eternal outward surge into an emptiness without limit. That was never a uniquely American vision, of course, though American culture fixated on it in predictable ways; a nation that grew up on the edge of vastness and cherished dreams of heading west and starting life over again was guaranteed to think of space, in the words of the *Star Trek* cliché, as "the final frontier." That it did indeed turn out to be our final frontier, the one from which we fell back at last in disarray and frustration, simply adds a mordant note to the tale.

It's crucial to realize that the fact that a dream is entrancing and appeals to our core cultural prejudices is no guarantee that it will come true, or even that it can. There will no doubt be any number of attempts during the twilight years of American empire to convince Americans to fling some part of the energies and resources that remain to them into a misguided attempt to relive the dream and claim some supposed destiny among the stars. That's not a useful choice at this stage of the game. Especially but not only in America, any response to the crisis of our time that doesn't start by using much less in the way of energy and resources simply isn't serious. The only viable way ahead for now, and for lifetimes to come, involves learning to live well within our ecological limits; it might also help if we were to get it through our heads that the Earth is not humanity's cradle, or even its home, but rather the whole of which each of us, and our species, is an inextricable part.

That being said, it is far from inappropriate to honor the failed dream that will shortly be gathering dust in museums and rusting in the winds that blow over Cape Canaveral. Every civilization has some sprawling vision of the future that's destined never to be fulfilled, and the dream of infinite expansion into space was ours. The fact that it didn't happen, and arguably never could have happened, takes nothing away from the grandeur of its conception, the passion, genius, and hard work that went into its pursuit, or the sacrifices made on its behalf. Some future poet or composer, perhaps, will someday gather it all up in the language of verse or music, and offer a fitting elegy to the age of space.

Meanwhile, some 240,000 miles from the room where I write this, a spidery metallic shape lightly sprinkled with meteoritic dust sits alone in the lunar night on the airless sweep of Mare Tranquillitatis. On it is a plaque which reads WE CAME IN PEACE FOR ALL MANKIND. Even if no other human eyes ever read that plaque again, as seems likely, it's a proud thing to have been able to say, and a proud thing to have done. I can only hope that the remembrance that our species once managed the thing offers some consolation during the bitter years ahead of us.

The Glass Bead Game

(Originally published 14 September 2011)

When I proposed in last week's *Archdruid Report* post that readers write science fiction stories about the crisis of industrial society,* I wasn't thinking of Fed chairman Ben Bernanke as a potential author. Still, a speech of his that made the New York Times a few days back suggests that he's got a sufficiently wild imagination for the job.

In that speech, while trying to explain why shoveling trillions of dollars of money into the coffers of the banks that caused the Great Recession hasn't done anything besides enriching bankers, Bernanke insisted that all that's wrong with the economy is that Americans are irrationally depressed about it. That, he claimed, is all that's keeping consumers from engaging in the binge spending that will get the economy moving again. You have to hand it to the man; it's an extraordinary leap of fantasy.

Out there in the real world, after all, a sixth of the US population is living below the poverty line. Most Americans who are still employed are taking steep cuts in salary and benefits where they aren't waiting day by day to see who gets a pink slip next. Then, of course, in a little over two years, Obama's health care legislation will place yet another massive burden on working people by requiring

---

* The best of these were collected and published as *After Oil: SF Visions of A Post-Petroleum World*).

them to buy health insurance whether they can afford it or not, at whatever price the industry chooses to charge for it, with only airy assurances of subsidies from a government already drowning in debt to balance against health insurance rates that are currently higher, for many families, than the monthly cost of the home they live in.

In other words, Americans are frantically paying off their debts, cutting their expenditures, downscaling their lifestyles, and trying to get some cash put by, because they have plenty of good reasons already to worry about their financial survival, and will have an even better one come 2014. It's tempting to add another reason for worry to the list—a political establishment, on both sides of the aisle, that's blatantly out of touch with reality—but there's more driving Bernanke's essay in science fiction than a simple case of common or garden variety cluelessness. The core issue, as I see it, is that the economy is not behaving the way economic theory says it ought to behave.

Among many other things, we've begun to see the first stirrings of stagflation—the theoretically impossible combination of a contracting economy and rising prices for necessities. That this round of stagflation follows the peak of world conventional crude oil production, just as the last round followed the peak of US crude oil production, is hardly an accident, but the connection is one that mainstream economic thought has an inborn inability to address. The dogma that demand creates supply, or more generally that financial forces can trump the laws of physics and geology, is so deeply ingrained in contemporary economics that the obvious connection between rising resource costs and economic malfunction is quite simply invisible to most of today's economists.

Bernanke's attempt to blame it all on an irrational epidemic of national gloominess will likely prove to be the first of many excuses we'll see over the years to come, as the mismatch between economic theory and the facts on the ground becomes harder and harder to ignore. Connoisseurs of imaginative fiction will want to keep an ear tuned to the utterances forthcoming from centers of power across the industrial world; we'll doubtless hear some whoppers. Still, I have to question whether any of this flurry of fantasy has much to offer as we rattle and bump down the rough roads on the far side of Hubbert's peak, and with that question in mind, I'd like to turn to a very different work of fiction that brings up some points the Ben Bernankes of the world seem most disposed to miss.

This is all the more interesting in that the work in question, though it's set in the future and makes some very subtle speculations about that future, doesn't seem to have been recognized as a science fiction novel at all. This was probably a good thing at the time, because it won its author a Nobel Prize for literature, and you don't get those for science fiction. Still, it seems to me that it's past time that the work I have in mind be assigned to its proper genre. The novel is *The Glass Bead Game*, and its author was Hermann Hesse.

When I first started college, Hesse's name was one to conjure with among the young and hip. He'd developed a cult following on American campuses about the same time J.R.R. Tolkien did, and for similar reasons; though the two authors differed in just about every other way you care to think of, both wove hard questions about the presuppositions of twentieth century industrial civilization into their fiction. Both were accordingly dismissed as unreadable by most Americans until the social changes of the late 1960s called those presuppositions into question. When the reaction set in during the 1980s, Tolkien's life's work was neatly gelded by being turned into raw material for an industry of derivative fantasy that borrowed all his imagery and none of his ideas, and tacitly ignored the hard questions he posed about the lust for power welded into the heart of modern technology. Hesse's novels were harder to stripmine for cheap clichés, and so in America, at least, they were simply forgotten.

Even in the days when every other college student you met had a copy of *Siddhartha* or *Steppenwolf* tucked in a garish backpack, though, *The Glass Bead Game*—for some reason, most American editions retitled it *Magister Ludi*—was a more rarefied taste. It's a very odd story: a hagiography, more or less, compiled by a bumbling and officious scholar in the early 25th century, about a controversial figure of the previous century whose deep ambiguities of character and action go right over the narrator's head. There are plenty of things that make it a more challenging read than some of Hesse's shorter and more popular novels, but I've come to think that one of those relates directly to the theme of this blog: the twenty-fourth century setting Hesse shows the reader in brief glimpses around the life of Magister Ludi Josephus II, aka Joseph Knecht, master of the Glass Bead Game, is not a twenty-fourth century that most people in the 1970s and early 1980s were willing to imagine.

It's one of the deft touches of the novel that Hesse paints that future with a very sparing brush, but the transition between our time and Joseph Knecht's gets explained in enough detail to make a definite kind of sense. The early twentieth century, in Hesse's future history, ushered in what later scholars would call the Age of Wars, a century-long period of prolonged and brutal violence that saw most of Europe repeatedly ravaged and the centers of global power shift decisively to other parts of the world. When lasting peace finally came, what was left of Europe tried to figure out what it was that drove the frenzy. The answer they settled on was the profound dishonesty and political prostitution of the intellectual life of the age—a time when, to quote a professor of the Age of Wars cited by Joseph Knecht in a letter, "Not the faculty but His Excellency the General can properly determine the sum of two and two."

In the postwar era, accordingly, the scholarly professions reorganized themselves on monastic lines as ascetic Orders, and each of the surviving European nations set aside a portion of land as a "pedagogic province," supported by the state but free from political interference, where talented youth could be educated, schoolteachers could be provided for the rest of the country, and scholars could pursue their research in relative security. Nearly the entire story of *The Glass Bead Game* takes place in one such region, Castalia, the pedagogic province of Switzerland. There and in equivalent provinces elsewhere, in the wake of the Age of Wars, the most gifted minds of each nation pursued research projects full time, and created a future...

If you were expecting that sentence to end "...of dramatic technological progress" or the like, think again. This is where Hesse's future history bounces right off the rails of our expectations, into territory that may seem surprisingly familiar to regular readers of this blog. It's worth remembering that science fiction of the more standard kind, with plenty of whiz-bang technology, was widely read in the central Europe Hesse knew. Nobody likes to talk much these days about pre-1945 central European science fiction, because a very large part of it enthusiastically pushed the aggressive authoritarian populism that got its lasting name from Mussolini's Fascist Party and helped launch the metastatic horror of Nazi Germany, but there was a lot of it, packed with the usual science fiction notions of endlessly accelerating social change driven by limitless technological advances. It's pretty clear that Hesse deliberately rejected those notions in his own work.

The future the busy scholars of Castalia create, rather, is a period of ordinary European history differing from earlier periods mostly in its lack of war. Technology, far from progressing, stabilized after the Age of Wars, and most modern machines seem less common than in our time. A trip by railway makes a brief appearance early on, but only that once. Automobiles exist, but only two of them appear in the story; one is owned by a wealthy and politically influential family, while the other is assigned to take a high official of the Castalian hierarchy to important meetings. Most of the time, when a character goes someplace and the mode of travel is mentioned at all, the trip is made on foot.

Other high technology isn't much more common. Broadcast

media, type not specified, play a minor role in the story at one or two points, and there's some kind of projection system that allows equations to appear on a large screen as they're being written, but that's about it. Doubtless astronomers have big telescopes and the like—Castalia has astronomers, yes, but it's the only science that Hesse mentions by name. Most of the scholars of the pedagogic province work in fields such as mathematics, musicology, philology and philosophy, or take part in the jewel in Castalia's crown, the Glass Bead Game.

The Game is arguably Hesse's greatest creation, a stunningly successful piece of social science fiction so far ahead of the conventions of the genre that its implications haven't even registered yet with other writers in the field. Unlike most modern thinkers, Hesse realized that historical periods value different intellectual projects; the contemporary conceit that treats technological progress as the most, or even the only, valid use of the human intellect is simply one more culturally and historically contingent judgment call, no more objectively true than the medieval belief that scholastic theology was the queen of the sciences. In twenty-fourth century Europe, attitudes have changed again, and an abstract contemplative discipline, half game and half art form, has become the defining cultural project of the time.

For reasons I'll develop in a forthcoming post, I want to take a moment here to talk a bit about the Game itself as Hesse envisioned it. It emerged, according to his invented history, out of the fields of mathematics and musicology, as scholars found common patterns underlying the two disciplines—the structure of a geometric proof, let's say, sharing the same abstract form as a Bach fugue or a Gregorian chant. Early on, the game was played with an abacus-like device with wires representing the conventional musical staff, and glass beads of different sizes, colors, shapes, and so on—thus the name of the Game—providing a more complex alphabet in place of simple musical notes. Later on, a formal mathematical script was developed; more scholarly disciplines took up the Game, finding their own abstract patterns and relating them to the musico-mathematic core; meditation exercises became part of the toolkit; public Games, attended by crowds, broadcast to large audiences, and surrounded by festivals of music and the arts, became major annual spectacles.

It's another of Hesse's defter touches that by the time of Joseph Knecht, the golden age of the Glass Bead Game is already past. Public Games that once extended for a month straight now run for two weeks at most, attended by smaller audiences and fewer public officials; the first stirrings of discontent about the funding allotted to Castalia and its equivalents are beginning to be heard; political events in the Far East have raised the specter of an end to the long period of European peace. How this plays out in the course of the story is something I'll leave to those of my readers who decide to try Hesse's novel for themselves, but it's not giving anything away to say that Hesse's sensitivity to the pace of historic change was a good deal keener than that of most other authors of science fiction.

There are two reasons I've chosen to discuss *The Glass Bead Game* here—well, three, counting the simple fact that it's an old favorite of mine that deserves more attention than it's gotten in recent decades. Aside from that, first of all, Hesse's future Europe may not quite be an ecotechnic society, but it's the kind of society that could exist and flourish in a future on the far side of peak oil. A nation or a continent in which automobiles are a rare and expensive luxury, railroads provide the bulk of what mechanized transport is needed, high technology is relatively scarce, and the values of society focus on pursuits that don't require burning up immense quantities of cheap energy, could probably get by tolerably well, and provide a decent standard of living to its population, in the absence of fossil fuels. At a time when most people can't conceive of a world that lacks our current glut of cheap abundant energy without turning immediately to the fantasies of squalor and savagery our culture habitually projects onto the inkblot patterns of the past, Hesse's novel suggests an alternative view—though he's quite clear, of course, that the route there leads through some very harsh territory.

The second reason follows from this, and heads in directions that will be as uncomfortable for many of my readers as it is unavoidable. It's pretty much standard practice for every society to assume that its particular tastes and values are universal truths, and to think that any society that doesn't share those tastes and values is by definition ignorant, or backward, or—well, you can fill in the putdown of your choice; there are plenty to go around. Our culture's obsession with replacing human capacities by machines is a case in point. It's very nearly unquestioned in modern industrial societies that getting a machine to do something that human beings would otherwise do is a good thing; even nations with crippling rates of unemployment persist in using a definition of productivity that amounts in practice to seeing how many people can be put out of work by replacing their labor with machines.

Our machine fetish, as I've discussed here more than once in the past, could only be indulged in so long as the extravagant use of fossil fuels made mechanical labor cheaper than human labor. That's already started to reverse—there are good reasons, after all, why most of the world's manufacturing is now done in Third World countries using cheap human labor rather than in the industrial world with expensive automated machines—but the cult of the machine retains much of its grip on our collective imagination. Even among those who recognize that the age of cheap energy is ending, the most common first reaction is to try to find some way to keep some favorite type of machine running—automobiles, the internet, the space program, you name it.

Among the most crucial tasks facing the pioneers of the deindustrial age, in turn, are those involved in slipping free of that now-obsolete mindset. Machines, as I think most of us have noticed by now, make very poor replacements for human beings, and the reverse is almost as true. Shifting from a machine society to a human society in the wake of peak oil, then, is not simply a matter of replacing one set of components with another that happen to be human. It's necessary to replace attitudes, values, and expectations that are suited to machines—and nearly the entire modern worldview can be summed up in these terms—with the very different attitudes, values, and expectations that produce good results when applied to human beings.

That leads in turn to issues that have been implicit in the project of this blog since its beginning more than five years ago, but that I've been doing my level best to avoid bringing up. At the core of these issues lies a topic so heavily loaded with ignorance and deliberate misunderstanding on all sides that it's seemed far wiser to leave it well alone. Still, if we're going to finish the project of exploring a toolkit for green wizards—a set of skills and a knowledge base suited to the crisis of industrial society and the hard work of beginning to build a new way of life while the old one is tottering around us—it can't be avoided any longer. For that reason, despite serious misgivings, I'm going to begin a series of posts next week that will talk about the relationship between peak oil and magic.[*]

---

[*] This series was the raw material for my book *The Blood of the Earth: An Essay on Magic and Peak Oil.*

Pepperspraying the Future

(Originally published 30 November 2011)

A whiff of pepper spray rising from a suburban big box store, a breathtakingly absurd comment by an American politician, a breathtakingly cynical statement from a Canadian minister: three scraps of data sent whirling down the wind unnoticed by most of today's disinformation society, which are also three clues to the exceptionally unwelcome future the industrial world is making for itself. Let's take them one at a time, in reverse order.

On Monday, as a new round of climate change talks got under way in Durban, Canadian environment minister Peter Kent confirmed earlier media reports that Canada will refuse to accept any further cuts in its carbon dioxide output under the Kyoto treaty. Since Canada is one of the few countries on Earth that uses more energy per capita than the United States—an impressive feat, really, when you think about it—you might be tempted to believe that there was room for some modest cuts, but that notion is nowhere in Kent's view of the universe. Those same media reports claimed that Canada was preparing to extract itself from the Kyoto treaty altogether; Kent dodged that question, but as Bob Dylan sang a good long time ago, you don't need to be a weatherman to know which way the wind is blowing.

The week before, in a debate among candidates for the GOP's presidential nomination, Newt Gingrich responded to a question about oil supplies by insisting that the United States could easily increase its oil production by four million barrels a day next year, if only those dratted environmentalists in the other party weren't getting in the way. This absurd claim was quickly and efficiently refuteded by several peak oil writers, but outside the peak oil blogosphere, nobody blinked. Never mind that the entire United States only produces 5.9 million barrels a day, that it took twenty years for the Alaska North Slope fields (peak production, 2 million barrels per day) to go from discovery to maximum output, or that the United States has been explored for oil more thoroughly than any other piece of real estate on the planet; the pundits and the public alike nodded and went on to the next question, as though a serious contender for the position of most powerful human being on the planet hadn't just gone on record claiming that two plus two is whatever you want it to be.

All of which brings us inevitably to a Los Angeles suburb on Thanksgiving, where a woman seems to have peppersprayed her fellow shoppers to get a video game console to put under her Christmas tree.

To be fair, the situation seems to have been a bit more complex than that sounds at first hearing. If you're still thinking of Thanksgiving Day in America in terms of lavish turkey dinners and visits from relatives, think again. Nowadays it serves mostly to mark the beginning of the year's big shopping season, and stores on the cutting edge of American marketing open their doors Thanksgiving night to give shoppers their first shot at whatever overpriced gewgaws the media has decreed will be the hot item this year. The store where the pepper spray incident happened was one of these. There, the mob that formed, waiting for the sale to start, turned unruly; there was apparently shoving and shouting, and then the pepper spray came out. According to witnesses, the woman who used it incapacitated enough of the competition to get to one of the video game consoles that were the center of the agitation, hurried off with it to a checkstand, bought the console and got away. Twenty people, some of them children, needed treatment by medics at the scene.

A fair amount of self-important clucking in the American media followed the incident, though I don't think anyone quite had the bad taste to point out that at least this year nobody was trampled to death by mobs of shoppers—yes, this happens every few years. Stephen Colbert, as usual, landed one in the bull's-eye by pointing out that the incident would make a great video game. He's right enough that I wouldn't be the least surprised if *Black Friday*, in which shoppers punch, spray, stab, and shoot each other to get choice gifts for Christmas, turns out to be the hot new video game sensation next year and inspires pepper sprayings and tramplings of its own.

What all these three news stories have in common is that they display an attitude—it could as well be described as a belief, or even a religion—that treats the satisfaction of short term cravings for material goods as the only thing that really matters. The shopper with her pepper spray, the politician with his absurd claim, and the government with its blind disregard for national survival, each acted as though *getting the stuff* is all that matters, and any obstacle in the way—whether the obstacle was other shoppers, the laws of physics and geology, or the fate of Canada's future generations—was an irrelevance to be brushed aside by any available means.

In recent years, there's been a fair amount of intellectual effort devoted to the attempt to prove that this is inevitably how human beings will act, and this effort has had an influence well beyond the borders of, say, cognitive neuroscience. Glance over anything the peak oil blogosphere has to say about the absurdity of today's public policies on energy, the environment, or the economy, for example, and it's a safe bet that somebody will post a comment insisting that this is how human beings always behave. In point of historical fact, though, this is far from true. The popularity of the monastic life across so many cultures and centuries is hard to square with such claims; it has not been uncommon for anything up to ten per cent of the population of some countries and times to embrace lives of poverty, celibacy and discipline in a monastic setting. Clearly, whatever drives push our species in the direction of the satisfaction of short term cravings are not quite as omnipotent as they've been made out to be.

More to the point, those of us who had the chance to get to know people of the generation that came of age in the Great Depression have a solid counterexample to mind. A great many Americans who lived through that long ordeal came out of the experience with a set of attitudes toward material goods that were radically different from the ones we've just been discussing. They were, to judge by the examples I had the chance to know, as materialistic as any other American generation has ever been, but the shadow of 1929 lay permanently across any notion that pursuing short term gains at the cost of long term disaster could possibly be a good idea. It's not accidental that the gutting of regulations on banks that made the current economic debacle possible did not happen until the generation that had witnessed 1929 had passed from public life—nor that it was the generation of the Baby Boom, the first to grow up after depression and war had definiteively given way to Pax Americana, that first put today's culture of short term satisfaction into overdrive.

The behavior of a society, in other words, has at least as much to do with its recent experience of the world as it does with the deeper but more diffuse influence of the biological drives its members share with the rest of the species. Ironically, Gingrich's response in the presidential debate pointed this up, though I suspect he himself will be the last person on the planet to realize this. He insisted that just as the United States was able to crush the Axis powers in the Second World War, a mobilization on a similar scale guided by the same optimism and can-do attitude could overwhelm any conceivable petroleum shortage and crash the price of oil. It's a common metaphor—how many times have people in the peak oil scene, for example, called for a new Manhattan Project?—but in the present context it's hopelessly misleading.

The Second World War, if anything, is a textbook case in what happens when optimism and a can-do attitude runs up against the hard facts of thermodynamics. All things considered, the Axis powers had better generalship, more disciplined military forces, and a much keener grasp of the possibilities of mechanized warfare than the Allies had at first, and Germany, at least, was ahead of the Allies in advanced military technology all the way through the war. What they did not have was secure access to fuel—and lacking that, they lost. Russia's Baku oilfields and the immense US petroleum deposits in Texas and elsewhere more than made up the difference, providing the Allies with practically limitless supplies of energy, and thus of troops, weapons, mobility, and everything else that makes for victory in war. Having those things, they won.

It's all the more ironic in that a similar struggle had a similar result on Gingrich's home turf a century and a half ago. No one can possibly accuse the Confederacy of a shortage of optimism or can-do attitude, and the chief Confederate generals were by and large better than their Union rivals. What those same Union generals finally figured out, though, was that the North's larger population and vastly greater economic base meant that generalship didn't matter; the North simply had to force the South into one meatgrinder battle after another, because even if the Union losses were larger, they could be replaced and the South's could not. Appomattox followed in due order.

One of the points that needs to be drawn from these examples, and the many others like them, is that optimism and a can-do attitude are in large part effects rather than causes; or, to put matters a little differently, they are relevant to certain circumstances and not to others. In the twentieth century, a nation with abundant supplies of coal, oil, and iron ore could well afford boundless optimism, and got along better with boundless optimism than without it, because the resource base was there to back up that optimism and give it muscles—and, when necessary, teeth. A nation that lacks such resources but still sets out to act on the basis of boundless optimism, on the other hand, risks ending up in roughly the same condition as the American South in 1865 or Germany and Japan in 1945. Such a nation needs to foster entirely different qualities than the ones just mentioned: circumspection, patience, and a keen sense of the downside risks of any opportunity come to mind. Equipped with these, it's possible for a nation with few resources to distract, dissuade, and ultimately outlast its potential enemies. That's the secret of Switzerland's survival, to cite one example among many.

The wild card in these calculations comes into play when shifts in technology, on the one hand, or the depletion of nonrenewable resources on the other, changes the status of a nation faster than its internal cultural shifts can adapt. Britain's history is a case in point. Britain's empire happened to come of age just as the Industrial Revolution was dawning, and coal—of which Britain had huge and easily accessible deposits—was the essential fuel of that revolution, powering the steam engines and (in the form of coke) the iron and steel foundries that were essential to economic and military power in the eighteenth and nineteenth centuries. With the dawn of the twentieth century, though, petroleum—far more energy-rich than even the best anthracite coal, and irreplaceable as fuel for gasoline and diesel engines, which were busy putting coal-fired steam power out of business—elbowed coal out of the way. Britain had next to no petroleum supplies of her own, since the offshore drilling techniques that made the North Sea fields accessible were still decades in the future.

The result was a tremendous new range of vulnerabilities that next to nobody noticed in time. Twice in twenty-five years, accordingly, Britain blundered into a land war in Europe and found itself abruptly scrambling for survival. In both cases, it had to turn to its erstwhile colony, the United States, to bail it out, and the price tag on those bailouts finally included Britain's empire and its status as a major world power. (There were several other countries just as eager as we were to buy Britain's empire and status, but the US—well, basically, we peppersprayed them and left the store with our prize.) Optimism and a can-do attitude counted for very little, for example, when German submarines could throw a noose around the British islands that Britain alone couldn't break.

The end of the age of petroleum promises another set of upsets on the same scale, but this time it's not because some more convenient and concentrated resource has suddenly come on the scene. It's because the world's production of conventional petroleum peaked in 2005 and has been declining ever since. A desperate scramble to fill the resulting gap with what appear on the charts as "other liquids"—ethanol, biodiesel, tar sand extracts, you name it, if it can be poured into a fuel tank and burnt, it gets counted—has filled in the gap, at least for now, but all these "other liquids" require much more energy to produce than ordinary petroleum does, and of course those energy inputs aren't accounted for in the totals. Thus, on paper, we've been chugging along a bumpy plateau for six years now, while in the real world—because of the rising energy inputs demanded by the "other liquids"—the supply of fuel available to do anything other than produce more fuel has been steadily sliding.

The problem we face right now is that it's only been a few short years since world petroleum production was expanding, and next to nobody has begun to think through the implications of the shift. Neither the United States nor anybody else has the vast supplies of energy and other raw materials that would be needed to back up the confident, brash optimism of an earlier day, and yet we still cling to the notion that those attitudes are the appropriate response to any crisis, because that's the approach we know. Patience, prudence, hard realism, the cold-eyed assessment of potential risks—those are foreign concepts to the leaders and the populace alike in most of the world's industrial nations, and especially so here in America, where the cult of enthusiastic optimism has been welded solidy in place since before the birth of the Republic. It has always worked before, and most Americans at every point on the socioeconomic spectrum are firmly convinced that it will work again.

But it will not work again, because the resources that would allow it to work again no longer exist.

That is why, dear reader, if you happen to live for another few decades, and have the chance to look back from that vantage point on the years just ahead of us, you are likely to see those years littered with the scraps of any number of grandiose plans meant to overcome the rising spiral of crises taking shape around us right now. None of them will have worked, because none of them will deal with the driving force behind that spiral of crisis—the hard fact that we've exhausted most of the easily extracted, highly concentrated energy sources on this planet, and are going to have to downscale our expectations and our collective sense of entitlement to fit within the narrower and more burdensome limits that dependence on renewable energy sources will impose on us. Quite the contrary; every one of these projects will start from the assumption that optimism and a can-do attitude can overcome those limits—and the tighter the limits press and the more obvious it becomes that the limits aren't budging, the more passionate the claims that one more heroic effort will defeat them once and for all.

Those claims will come from every point on the political spectrum, and will wrap themselves in every conceivable scrap of rhetoric that comes to hand. Before all this is over, I expect to see people who now call themselves environmentalists advocating for the stripmining of our national parks—in an environmentally sensitive manner, to be sure. We've already seen erstwhile environmentalists such as Stewart Brand and George Monbiot championing nuclear power; how poisoning the biosphere with radioactive waste makes more sense than flooding the atmosphere with carbon dioxide may well puzzle you as much as it does me, but straining at greenhouse gnats and swallowing nuclear camels is apparently a job requirement in their field these days.

What neither the pundits nor the politicians nor ordinary people are willing to consider, in turn, is the one option that offers a meaningful way forward: learning the old and necessary lesson that our desires need to be held within the bounds that the universe provides for us, and that long term goals and values need to trump short term cravings, especially where material goods are concerned. We can no longer afford the sort of attitude that insists that it's okay to pepperspray our fellow shoppers to get that brand new video game console, or pepperspray the laws of physics and geology to get that extra four million barrels a day of oil (or, more precisely, to get the presidency by pretending we can get that extra four million barrels a day of oil), or pepperspray Canada's grandchildren to get the right set of pretty figures on the national balance of trade and federal budget. Still, for the foreseeable future, pepperspray will be popular in the corridors of power and the corner tavern alike, and it will take a certain number of unnecessary disasters before that ends and people in the industrial world begin to come to terms with the new reality.

This, finally, is why I've spent the last year and a half passing on what I learned, decades ago, of the do-it-yourself green wizardry of the Seventies, and why I've supplemented that over the last two months with some of the basic elements of magic—the art and science of causing change in consciousness in accordance with will—which I also began to learn in the Seventies, and which had rather more than a nodding acquaintance in those days with the movements focused on appropriate technology, organic gardening, and the rest of it. During the years immediately ahead of us, unless I'm very much mistaken, the political, economic, and cultural institutions of the industrial world can be counted on to do just about anything other than a meaningful response to the crisis of our age, and any meaningful response that does happen is going to have to come from individuals, families, and community groups.

During those same years, I suspect, every available effort will be made to convince as many people as possible that the nonsolutions on offer are actually meaningful responses, and the things that might actually help—using less, conserving more, and downscaling our burden on the planet—are unthinkable. That's the sort of thing that happens when the world changes, and structures and institutions adapted to an old reality turn out to be hopelessly unworkable in the new one. Next week we'll talk about what might follow that period, and wrap up the discussion of green wizardry and magic alike for the time being.

Waiting for the
Great Pumpkin
(Originally published 4 January 2012)

With the coming of the new year, predictions of what's in store during the next twelve months are showing up here and there in the peak oil blogosphere: a feature of the season, really, as reliable as the icicles that hang from the roof's edge outside the window of my study. Like the icicles, they're enticing to look at; like the icicles, equally, a great many of them are guaranteed to drop to the ground and shatter at some point in the months to come.

That's all the more remarkable in that, by and large, the peak oil community has been pretty much spot on when it comes to the general shape of the future. Five or ten years ago, it bears remembering, nobody else was predicting the sustained oil prices on the far side of $100 a barrel and the global economic gridlock that have become fixtures of the contemporary scene; the peak oil scene had that one nailed. A healthy skepticism toward whatever the current speculative bubble happens to be—tech stocks back in the days when the peak oil blogosphere was first getting under way, real estate in the runup to the 2008 crash, shale gas and shale oil now— has also been a common feature in the peak oil scene throughout its history, even when almost everyone else was cheering along the bubble du jour as the wave of the future.

Why, then, all the annual predictions that misfire—and in

particular, why the *same* annual predictions that have misfired for years in a row? Why, for example, the relentless annual round of claims that the coming year will finally see a sudden and total economic collapse? That one's been made time and again, often by the same bloggers, and the fact that each year goes by without anything of the kind happening somehow never manages to affect the next year's confident insistence that this time around the wolves really, truly are about to eat all the sheep. It would be funny, really, except that pointing out the long string of failed predictions has become a standard rhetorical trick in the arsenal of those—either madmen or economists, to use Kenneth Boulding's useful taxonomy—who want to insist on the possibility of limitless growth on a finite planet.

Now of course it's only fair to point out that there are at least as many predictions on the other side of the picture that are still being recycled this year after an equivalent track record of failures. Hope springs eternal—or, rather, the facile optimism of the privileged that masquerades as hope in too much of contemporary culture springs infernal—in the minds of the many bloggers who expect some shiny new technological gimmick to overturn the laws of thermodynamics and give us a glossy new future straight out of *The Jetsons*. The technological savior du jour, to be sure, changes even faster than the bubble du jour; we've seen ethanol, big wind turbines, and now shale gas touted as game-changing developments; neither ethanol nor wind turbines changed much of anything, of course, but when shale gas lands in the same category—as it will—there will be another candidate for the role

For that matter, those who insist that petroleum can't run out because we want it so badly have had just as dubious a record, if not more so. I've reminded my readers several times already about Daniel Yergin's 2004 prediction that new petroleum discoveries would keep the price of crude oil at a plateau of $38 a barrel, and he's far from the only pundit who's made claims that absurd and still had the media fawning at his feet. More generally, have you noticed that every couple of years, we get to hear some new claim that a vast new oil discovery somewhere is about to solve the world's energy troubles? They're as regular as clockwork or, these days, as speculative bubbles; the actual results, once the hype gives way to the business end of a drilling bit, range from modest to none at all; still, none of that slows down the missionaries of the religion of limitless petroleum.

It's all uncomfortably reminiscent of the *Peanuts* character Linus, with his enduring faith that this year, despite all previous disconfirmations, the Great Pumpkin really will show up with candy for all on Halloween. Still, as I look back over the last dozen years or so, I notice a feature common to the predictions I'm discussing that Linus' lonely vigil in the pumpkin patch doesn't share. Is it just me, or do my readers also catch the note of increasing desperation in a good many of the latest round of familiar predictions?

On the cornucopian side of the picture, certainly, that note is hard to miss. One measure of this is the extent to which the most remarkable evasions of fact have been finding their way into the media of late when the subject of US energy production comes up. The example I'm thinking of just now is the claim, recycled by any number of supposedly serious pundits in the last few months, that the United States has become a net exporter of petroleum. As it happens this is—well, let's be polite and call it an inaccuracy; a less courteous though arguably more accurate phrase would be "bald-faced lie." The US last year imported around two-thirds of the crude oil it used, just as it did the year before, and exported very little crude oil. Follow the footnotes, though, and they lead in interesting directions.

What has happened over the last few years, in fact, is that the US has become a net exporter of refined petroleum products. For many years before then, along with the vast floods of crude oil shipped in from abroad to feed domestic refineries, the United States imported a modest amount of petroleum products that had been refined overseas, and shipped a smaller amount of its own refineries' products to other countries. As the current depression has tightened its grip on the country, though, consumption of gasoline and other petroleum products has dropped by more than ten per cent, and US refineries have found it profitable to sell more of their products overseas as the domestic market contracted. The total shift is not that large, and since what's driving it is the ongoing contraction of the US economy, it might be better treated as a warning sign than a reason for fatuous misstatements.

Still, beyond the misinformation and disinformation, fatuous and otherwise, there's a common thread running through all the various predictions I'm discussing here, and it's a thread worth tracing. All of them—the claims that a crash is imminent, or that a technological breakthrough is imminent, or that an abundant new source of fossil fuels is imminent, or what have you—are at bottom claims that the troubled situation in which the industrial world currently finds itself can't continue in anything like its present form. I'd like to offer instead the counterintuitive suggestion that it can, and most likely will.

What that would mean in practice can best be judged by thinking back a year or two, to the early days of 2011. The year that had just ended was a troubled time, with political turmoil, economic crises, a larger than usual number of natural disasters, and a pervasive (and in many cases quite accurate) sense on the part of many people that life was getting tougher and the solutions being offered by politicians weren't solving much of anything. Once we got past the annual flurry of predictions about game-changing events of one kind or another, what actually happened? The game didn't change at all. Instead, each of the difficulties I've just noted got a little worse. There was more political turmoil; the economic crises became somewhat more frequent and more severe; the number of natural disasters went up again—there were, as I recall, 32 weather-related disasters causing more than US$1 billion each in damages, which is a new record—and across the industrial world, people's faith in their government's capacity to do much of anything declined further.

That's what happened in 2011. I'd like to suggest that when we take a backwards look in the early days of 2013, we will most likely see that that's what happened in 2012, too: a slow worsening across a wide range of trends, punctuated by localized crises and regional disasters. I'd like to predict, in fact, that when we take that backward look, the US dollar and the Euro will both still exist and be accepted as legal tender, though the Eurozone may have shed a couple of countries who probably shouldn't have joined it in the first place; that stock markets around the world will have had another volatile year, but will still be trading. Here in the US, whoever is unlucky enough to win the 2012 presidential election will be in the middle of an ordinary transition to a new term of office; the new Congress will be gearing up for another two years of partisan gridlock; gas stations will still have gas for sale and grocery stores will be stocked with groceries; and most Americans will be making the annual transition between coping with their New Year's hangovers and failing to live up to their New Year's resolutions, just as though it was any other year.

That is to say, nothing much will have changed, if by the word "change" you mean exclusively the kind of dramatic break with the existing pattern of things that so many people are predicting just now. From any other perspective, plenty will have changed. Official US statistics will no doubt insist that the unemployment rate has gone down—do you ever get the feeling that when the Soviet Union collapsed, the people who used to churn out all those preposterous propaganda claims for their government got hired by ours? I do—but the number of people out of work in the United States will likely set another all-time record; the number of people in severe economic trouble will have gone up another good-sized notch, and public health clinics will probably be seeing the first wave of malnutrition-caused illness in children. If you happen to have spent the year in one of the areas unfortunate enough to get hit by the hard edge of the increasingly unstable weather, you may have had to spend a week or two in an emergency shelter while the flood waters receded or the wreckage got hauled away, and you might even notice that less and less gets rebuilt every year.

Unless that happens, though, or unless you happen to pay close attention to the things that don't usually make the evening news, you may well look back in the first days of 2013 and think that business as usual is still ongoing. You'd be right, too, so long as you recognize that there's been a stealthy change in what business as usual now means. Until the peak of world conventional petroleum production arrived in 2005, by and large, business as usual meant the continuation of economic growth. Since then, by and large, it has meant the continuation of economic decline.

And the repeated predictions that the situation can't go on? I've come to think that what motivates such predictions, and gives them their present popularity, is the growing sense of apprehension that it *can* go on—that the troubles currently pressing in on the industrial world could just keep on getting worse, day after day, year after year, for decades to come, following the same gradual curve that the industrial world followed in the days of its growth, but in reverse: descending into impoverishment and relocalization along some broad equivalent of the same bumpy course that brought the ascent to prosperity and global integration back in the day.

When you think about it—and in the back of their minds, I suspect, most people have thought about it—that's really a terrifying prospect. What makes it most unnerving is that it's not simply a matter of, say, having your standard of living ratchet down by five per cent every year, though there will be a fair amount of that. It's far more a matter of never knowing when your number's going to come up and land you out of work, out of money and out on the street, next to the others who landed there before you. How much of the popular sport of blaming the poor for their poverty, I wonder, and how much of the current pseudoconservative fad of insisting that the poor aren't actually poor, comes from people who are desperately trying to convince themselves that their jobs are irreplaceable, their retirement funds secure, and the sudden dizzying fall into the ranks of the impoverished can't possibly happen to them?

If the downward arc of business as usual in an age of decline is what we're facing, though, that sort of tortured logic is a pretty fair guarantee of final failure. The only way out of the trap, as I've argued here rather more than once, is to accept a steep cut in your standard of living before it becomes necessary, as a deliberate choice, and to use the resources freed up by that choice to get rid of any debts you have, get settled in a location that has a fair chance of keeping a viable degree of community life going, and get the tools and learn the skills that you will need to manage a decent life in an age of spiraling decline. To those who cling to the idea that they can maintain their present lifestyles, admittedly, it's hard to think of any advice less welcome, but the universe is in no way obligated to give us the future we want—even if what we want is a sudden blow that will spare us the harder experience of the Long Descent.

The Blood of the Earth, or Pulp Nonfiction

(Originally published 11 January 2012)

Some of my readers have wondered aloud why it is that I've devoted so much time in recent weeks to the current flurry of 2012 prophecies and their close equivalents. One reason is that there's good reason to think that we're going to hear quite a bit more about these prophecies in the months to come; unless I miss my guess, the apocalyptic bubble that's inflating now, and will pop this coming December 22, is going to be one for the record books. Still, there's at least one more reason to pay close attention to that bubble just now.

It's not often remembered these days that the literal meaning of the word "apocalypse" is the revelation of something hidden. The term got its modern meaning because most of the prophecies that have been so labeled claim to reveal one hidden thing in particular, that is, the imminent end of history; but there's another sense in which the word is even more appropriate, and that sense seems worth exploring just at the moment. The presence and popularity of apocalyptic beliefs, I've come to think, reveal something important about any society in which such beliefs occur.

Apocalyptic thinking, after all, doesn't come out of nowhere. It has an extensive history behind it, a point I tried to make in my recent book *Apocalypse Not,* but it also has roots in the collective psychology of any society in which it becomes popular. Epochs

119

awash in apocalyptic beliefs are also full of intense social stress, but there are stressful periods in which very few people spend their time feverishly getting ready for the end of the world. What seems to do the trick is a particular kind of stress—specifically, the kind that happens when the narratives a society uses to make sense of the world no longer work.

I've talked more than once in these essays about the immense role that narratives play in our mental and social lives. As human beings, we think with stories as inevitably as we eat with mouths and walk with feet; the stories we tell ourselves about the world define the way we make sense of the "blooming, buzzing confusion," in William James' phrase, that the world out there throws at our sense organs. In what we are pleased to call "primitive societies," a rich body of mythology and legend provides each person with a range of narratives that can be applied to any given situation and make sense of it. Learning the stories, and learning how to apply them to life's events, is the core of a child's education in these societies, and a learned person is very often distinguished, more than anything else, by the number of traditional stories he or she knows by heart.

More technologically advanced societies often, though not invariably, move away from this, consigning their inheritance of stories to children—think, for example, of the role of fairy tales in nineteenth- and twentieth-century industrial societies—while narrowing down the range of stories adults are supposed to think with, until all that's left are variations on one narrative. Serious thinking in these societies is by definition thinking that follows the accepted narrative. To be a respectable thinker in the heyday of the Roman Empire, for example, was by definition to filter the world through a narrative that described how original chaos was reduced to order, peace and prosperity under the paternal rule of a benevolent despot. Roman religion applied that narrative to the cosmos, Roman philosophy applied it to the relation between mind and body, and so on. The difficulty, of course, came when the world started throwing things at the Roman world that couldn't be made to fit the narrative.

We're in much the same situation today. Our core narrative, the story into which every serious thinker is required to fit his or her thoughts, is the narrative of progress—the story that defines all of human existence as a single great upward trajectory from the caves to the stars, and insists that the present is better than the past and the future will inevitably be better still. The problem with that narrative, of course, is that for most people the present is significantly worse than the past—standards of living for most Americans, for example, have been declining for more than thirty years—and the future promises to be even worse than the present. The narrative of progress has no room for that perception; in public life, the only way in which it's possible to bring it up at all is to suggest that someone or something is to blame for the temporary lack of progress, and then offer a plan to get the obstacle out of the way so that progress can get under way once more.

Politicians, pundits, and serious thinkers of every kind have been making exactly this argument for a good many decades, though, and it's started to sink in across a very broad range of the social spectrum that something has gone very wrong. There have been, so far, two main responses to this recognition. The surge in apocalyptic prophecies is one of them; the logical response when one narrative fails to make sense of the world is to look for another narrative that does a better job, after all, and the narrative of apocalypse—more precisely, the religious narrative of paradise, fall, and redemption in which apocalyptic prophecy has its natural habitat—is one of the very few alternatives that most people in industrial societies are willing to take seriously.

The second response to the recognition that the narrative of progress has failed is to rehash it over again in an even more extreme form. The poster child for this second option just now is a video titled *Thrive*, which is doing the rounds in the alternative scene as I write this. Those of my readers who are connoisseurs of meretricious nonsense may find it of interest, but I wouldn't recommend it to anyone else; we will all be hearing far too much like it over the years to come.

The basic message of *Thrive* is that we all ought to be living in a wonderful Utopian world, and would be doing so if evil corporate conspiracies weren't suppressing the inventions that would have given us limitless free energy, cures for cancer and, well, pretty much anything else your heart desires. Evidence? We don't need no steenking evidence—and of course, in an entirely pragmatic sense, *Thrive* doesn't; all it has to do is hammer over and over again on a set of emotional hot buttons until the viewer's ability to reason is overwhelmed, and if the video fails at this, it's certainly not for want of trying. It's a pity, in a way, that *Thrive* wasn't yet in circulation when I wrote last year's posts on thaumaturgy; it would have been educational to go through it scene by scene and talk about the crassly manipulative tactics it uses to get its effect.

Anyone interested in a thorough critique of *Thrive* should read Rob Hopkins' cogent essay[*] on the subject. For our present purposes, the point I want to make is that *Thrive* is an all-out effort to uphold the narrative of progress in the teeth of the facts. The narrative of progress says that we ought to have cheaper, more abundant energy with every passing year; in fact, the industrial world's supplies of cheap abundant energy are running out fast, with predictable effects on price and supply, but those effects and their causes simply can't be squared with the narrative of progress. Enter a flurry of accusations of conspiracy, which make it possible to insist that progress is still continuing but its fruits are being withheld from the people. The claims that cures for cancer are being suppressed has the same role with regard to the ongoing collapse of public health in America and elsewhere: we ought to be getting healthier, but we're not, so a scapegoat has to be found to justify the widening gap between the narrative we prefer and the reality we get.

---

[*]   http://transitionculture.org/2012/01/09/film-review-why-thrive-is-best-avoided/

For all the problems with apocalyptic thinking, then, the prophets of apocalypse have at least gotten the first step right; having noticed that the narrative of progress doesn't work anymore, they've gone looking for an alternative, and it's simply their bad luck that the alternative they've chosen doesn't work either. Of course that raises a challenging question: if the narratives of progress and apocalypse don't fit the world in which we're living or the future that's looming ahead of us, what narratives do?

Mulling over this question a few days ago, I started making a list of the more obvious features of the story in which we find ourselves at this point in the turning of history's wheel. I encourage my readers to follow along, and see whether or not the answer that struck me occurs to them as well.

- We live in a world dominated by a vast, slowly decaying empire that gets quite literally superhuman powers by feeding on what we may as well call the blood of the Earth;

- That empire is ruled by a decadent aristocracy that holds court in soaring towers and bolsters its crumbling authority by conjuring vast amounts of wealth out of thin air;

- Backing the aristocracy is a caste of corrupt sorcerers whose incantations, projected into every home through the power of the blood of the Earth, keep the populace disorganized, deluded and passive;

- Entire provinces of the empire are ravaged by droughts, storms, and other disasters caused by the misuse of the Earth's blood, while prophecies from the past warn of much worse to come;

- Meanwhile, far from the centers of power, the members of a scattered fellowship struggle to find and learn the forgotten lore of an earlier time, which might just hold the secret of survival...

It was more or less at this point that the realization hit: we have somehow gotten stuck, all seven billion of us, inside the pages of a pulp fantasy novel.

Those of my readers who are significantly younger than I am, and missed the vast outpouring of cheap fantasy novels that played so large and disreputable a role in shaping my youthful imagination, may benefit from a bit of history here. The runaway success of J.R.R. Tolkien's trilogy *The Lord of the Rings* in the late 1960s inspired publishers, who are after all in business to make money, to look for ways to cash in on the same market. One obvious gambit was to dredge up older fantasy fiction, and much of what was readily available was the pulp fantasy of the 1920s and 1930s, when H.P. Lovecraft's overheated prose and Robert Howard's overheated gonads filled the pages of *Weird Tales* magazine and the imagination of teenage America with musclebound barbarian heroes, tentacled horrors from three weeks before the beginning of time, and most of the other modern conveniences that have furnished fantasy fiction ever since.

Lovecraft and Howard were, alas, both dead when the late-Sixties fantasy explosion arrived, and so their ability to produce new works was somewhat limited. For a while, accordingly, it was possible for almost anybody who could write a literate English sentence to get into print as a fantasy novelist. Most of what flooded onto bookstore shelves in the years that followed was remarkably atrocious, with two-dimensional characters, engagingly bad prose, and utterly unconvincing plots duking it out in a loser-take-all contest. At the time, I wasn't a stickler about quality—I was in the market for anything more colorful than the two-dimensional blandness of an American suburban childhood—but I did prefer those who could write well; Tolkien's trilogy was one of those favorites, and so were the products of the busy pen of Michael Moorcock.

These days Moorcock counts as a serious novelist, having clambered up out of the mosh pit of pulp fantasy fiction into the rarefied balconies of literature. Back in the day, though, he was among the leading figures in the pulp fantasy revival. Better than any of his rivals, perhaps, Moorcock recaptured the flavor of the gloriously trashy *Weird Tales* era, penning sprawling sagas about a succession of heroes who were all iterations of one Eternal Champion, destined to hack his way forever through an infinity of parallel worlds. And the backgrounds against which Elric of Melniboné and Corum Jhaelen Irsei and Dorian Hawkmoon and the rest of them suffered, swaggered and fought? More often than not, they were vast and crumbling empires propped up by supernatural powers, ruled by decadent aristocrats who conjured various things out of thin air, full of corrupt sorcerers, whole provinces ravaged by disasters, and—well, I suspect you get the point by now.

Aside from the colorful details just mentioned, though, there was something else woven into the pulp fantasy of that era, Moorcock's and otherwise. The worlds of pulp fantasy are by and large worlds in decline, strewn with immense ruins and scattered with artifacts no one can duplicate any more. The heroes of pulp fantasy are caught up in the undertow of decline, and their battles and quests are generally defined by legacies of the pre-decline past that have to be preserved or destroyed before the future can begin to take shape. Interestingly, that was as often true in the *Weird Tales* era; Conan the Barbarian, who was placed by his creator Robert Howard somewhere in the conveniently undocumented past between the fall of Atlantis and the beginning of recorded history, spent much of his time dealing with the half-remembered legacies of the assorted drowned continents that Howard borrowed from Theosophical literature.

J.R.R. Tolkien, whose name I've invoked a couple of times already in this essay, worked with the same theme. There's been a great deal of literary criticism of Tolkien's work down through the years, but I don't recall seeing any that's talked about the extent to which Middle-earth was influenced by the pulp fantasy of the 1920s and 1930s, which Tolkien (like his friend C.S. Lewis) read eagerly. One of the things that makes Tolkien's work so inventive is the way that he plopped a bunch of hopelessly middle-class Englishmen dressed as hobbits into a world full of pulp fantasy clichés, complete with heroic survivors of drowned Atlantis—excuse me, Númenor— and an evil wizard-king who rides a tame pterodactyl into battle. Framing this arguably satiric dimension and the story as a whole there is, once again, the theme of decline: the twilight of the elves, the last hurrah of the heirs of Númenor, and the end of a sad and tangled story that had been winding down since the Elder Days. Middle-Earth is not a place where progress happens, any more than Conan's Hyborian Age or age of the Young Kingdoms in which Elric wielded the black sword Stormbringer.

A brand of fiction commonly dismissed as sheer escapism, in other words, provides narratives more useful to the current state of the industrial world than the supposedly serious narrative of progress that still shapes every detail of contemporary public discourse. I'm not sure how far to take that point, though I have to admit that if Mabelrode the Faceless, Demon Lord of Chaos, were to be named as CEO of Citibank, I'm not sure I would be surprised. (On the other hand, maybe he already has been; it would explain a few things.) It would arguably have been better for us all if, when Edwin Drake and his men went to drill the first commercial oil well at Titusville, Pennsylvania back in 1859, they had found an ominous standing stone there carved with glowing runes:

THE BLACK GOLD IS THE BLOOD OF THE EARTH
THE FORCE IN THE BLOOD IS THE FLAME OF THE SUN
TO DRINK OF THE BLOOD IS TO MASTER THE WORLD
BUT THE FATE OF THE EARTH AND ITS BLOOD ARE ONE

Still, we missed that warning, and so have never quite gotten around to noticing that the world around us has much more in common with pulp fantasy fiction than it does with what passes for serious thought these days.

By this point, though, I suspect that you, dear reader, are wondering about one detail. If we're actually stuck inside the pages of a trashy fantasy novel, as I've suggested, and all the details of the setting and the plot are in place, where is the protagonist? Who is the hero or the heroine who will turn the pages of the long-lost Gaianomicon, use its forgotten lore to forge a wand of power out of the rays of the Sun, shatter the deceptive spells of the lords of High Finance, and rise up amidst the wreckage of a dying empire to become one of the seedbearers of an age that is not yet born?

Why, you are, of course.

Night Thoughts in Hagsgate

(Originally published 23 May 2012)

There are times, at least for me, when the fate in store for industrial society can be seen with more than the usual clarity. I'm thinking just now of the time I looked out a train window and saw an abandoned factory, not yet twenty years old, with foot-high saplings rising incongruously from the gutter around the roof; or of another time, in a weekend flea market here in Cumberland, when I found a kid's book on space travel I'd loved as a child, flipped through the pages, and found myself face to face with the gap between the shining future we were supposed to have by now and the mess that was actually waiting for us when we got here.

I'm pondering another of those moments now, but the trigger this time isn't a trackside glimpse or a memento in a repurposed warehouse. It's the current flood of news stories, opinion pieces, and public statements by pundits of various kinds, all focused on one theme—the supposed irrelevance of peak oil.

Those of my readers who have managed to miss that torrent so far may find it helpful to spare a glance at this typical example of the species,[*] which was forwarded to me by one of this blog's readers (tip of the archdruidical hat to Hereward). The author, Timothy Worstall, is a senior fellow at the Adam Smith Institute in London,

---

[*] http://blogs.telegraph.co.uk/finance/timworstall/100017130/can-we-please-just-declare-the-death-of-peak-oil-and-start-worrying-about-something-important/

and a specialist in rare earth elements; he starts off by complaining that he doesn't understand peak oil, goes on to demonstrate that fact in impressive detail, and finishes up with the sort of whopper that normally earns an F on a freshman paper in Geology 101. (No, Mr. Worstall, kerogen shales such as the Green River formation are not at all the same thing as oil-bearing shales such as the Bakken formation, and nobody yet has a viable way to extract oil from kerogen shales; I trust you provide better information to clients who ask your advice about rare earth elements.)

I wish I could say that this is an extreme example, but it's not. Worstall has at least grasped the fact that peak oil has to do the rate at which oil can be produced, which is more than most critics of the concept manage, and his confusion between kerogen shales and oil-bearing shales—though it could have been cleared up by five minutes of research—is common among people who are poorly informed about petroleum geology. Look at other efforts to dismiss peak oil and you'll find worse. The question I'd like to raise is why this outpouring of misinformation and denial happens to be in full flood right now.

It's a very odd time for peak oil to be dismissed, all things considered. Back in the late 1990s, when the first peak oil researchers began to exchange data and forecasts, several leading figures in the newborn movement made very straightforward predictions about what was going to happen. They predicted that global production of crude oil would peak in the near future, and decline thereafter; they predicted that this would cause the price of oil and petroleum products to skyrocket, imposing severe costs on the global economy and triggering economic contraction; some, though this was controversial, predicted that attempts to replace petroleum with alternative energy sources would fail because of net energy and other noneconomic factors.

These assertions were rejected with quite some heat by the few people outside the scene who bothered to notice. Critics of peak oil insisted, first, that increasing demand for petroleum would make additional capital available for the hunt for new oil fields, which would of course be found, and thus allow petroleum production to grow indefinitely; second, that if the price of oil did rise sharply, that would simply make other energy sources viable, releasing a flood of energy onto the market that would drive prices back down; and third, that human ingenuity, the free market, or some other allegedly omnipotent force would certainly be able to find limitless new energy resources and prove all the pessimists wrong.

A decade and a half later, it's instructive to see how those predictions turned out. The short form is that the peak oil researchers were correct while their critics were shoveling smoke. The production of conventional crude oil peaked in 2005; the price of oil spiked to levels that pundits insisted it could never reach, and has moved raggedly upward since the initial spike and crash to today's value well above $100 a barrel; the global economy proceeded to lurch into serious trouble, and remains in a state of perpetual crisis that nobody in charge seems to be able to understand or fix; and a series of boomlets in hydrogen, ethanol, algal biodiesel and other much-hyped alternative energy sources rose and crashed as it turned out that no matter what oil cost, they cost more.

The current bubble in shale gas is to some extent an exception to that last rule, but it's hardly the bonanza that the media likes to claim. Partly, shale gas production is simply a side effect of the fact that natural gas liquids, which occur in some shale gas deposits, can be sold as a petroleum substitute at very good prices; partly, shale gas has morphed in recent years into what Wall Street aficionados call a pump-and-dump operation—a bit of dubious marketing in which operators boost the price of a stock, then sell it at the inflated price to suckers, who are sure the price will go up further and are therefore left holding the bag when it goes down instead. (I trust none of my readers have put their life savings into shale gas companies.)

Still, there's another factor to the shale gas bubble, and also to the boom in oil-bearing shale that has filled so many glowing headlines in recent years, and will fill so many gloomy headlines a few years further on. Both are being ballyhooed as game-changing breakthroughs, even though they're nothing of the kind— hydrofracturing ("fracking") has been a common practice for forty years, and the Bakken shale was discovered long ago. The fracking boom is simply one of the many ways in which the world is scraping low-grade fuels out of the bottom of the barrel, just as peak oil researchers have predicted it would. Their breakthrough status is entirely a product of hype. Behind that hype, I've come to think, and the comparable hype that surrounded the hydrogen economy, corn ethanol, and all the other failed pseudosolutions to our predicament, lies a very specific motive: the desire to find some reason, however fatuous, to insist that it's all right to keep on wallowing in the benefits of today's wildly unsustainable energy and resource consumption, instead of getting ready for the far less lavish world that's going to follow in short order.

That motive shapes a dizzyingly large share of the collective conversation of our time. Consider the book review I critiqued in last week's post.* One of the bits of rhetoric the reviewer used to dismiss my suggestion that social change has to be founded in personal change was the claim that "you can't end rape [just] by not raping anyone." Perhaps so, but as one of my readers pointed out (tip of the archdruidical hat here to Ozark Chinquapin), someone who claimed to oppose rape would normally be expected to demonstrate that commitment by, at the very least, not raping anyone; an antirape movement that claimed that rapes committed by its members didn't matter, because it was working to end rape everywhere, would rightly be dismissed as an exercise in extreme hypocrisy. Yet you'll hear the identical logic from people in a good deal of the environmental movement, who insist that they can't be bothered to

---

* http://dgrnewsservice.org/2012/05/04/book-review-the-blood-of-the-earth/

lighten the burden their lifestyles place on the planet because they're going to save the Earth all at once.

Work out the practical implications of that argument, in other words, and it amounts to a justification for clinging to the comforts and privileges of the modern industrial lifestyle even at the expense of one's supposed ideals. That's also the implication of the denunciations of peak oil I discussed at the beginning of this post, of course, and there are plenty of other ways of cloaking that same desire. Whether you expect solar power, thorium reactors, algal biodiesel or some other exciting new energy source to save the day; whether you anticipate the imminent arrival of the Rapture, the Singularity, the Space Brothers, a world-ending cataclysm, or a great leap of consciousness to some higher plane; or whether you simply tell yourself, as so many Americans do these days, "I'm sure they'll think of something"—if you look at that belief honestly, dear reader, doesn't it work out to an excuse that lets you claim that it really is okay for you to keep enjoying whatever you see as your share of the goodies churned out by the industrial machine?

It's here, in turn, that I glance down and see the void opening up beneath the foundations of that same machine—and it's also here that I find myself remembering a harrowing detail from one of the favorite books of my teen years, Peter Beagle's brilliant fantasy *The Last Unicorn*.

I'm not even going to try to sketch out the plot of the book as a whole. The point that's relevant here centers on a place, the town of Hagsgate, and its people, who are very rich. They live in the kingdom ruled by King Haggard, the villain of the story; they profit mightily from his rule, and are exquisitely careful not to notice anything that bears too closely on the terrifying evil that lies at the heart of his realm. They are also, as it happens, under a witch's curse.

It occurs to me that some of my readers may not be familiar with the structure and function of curses. (What *do* they teach children these days?) The sort of thing you get in bad modern remakes of fairy tales, where someone inoffensive gets burdened with a dire fate that would not otherwise befall them, is strictly amateur stuff. Professionals know that the curses that matter are the kind that unfold by their own inexorable logic from the actions and attitudes of the accursed. The witch or wizard who finds it necessary or appropriate to pronounce a curse doesn't have to make anything happen; he or she simply says aloud the unmentionable realities of the situation, states the necessary consequences, and leaves. The efforts of the accursed to avoid falling victim to the curse, without actually changing the things that make the curse inevitable, then proceed to drive the curse to its fulfillment.

The witch who cursed Hagsgate was a thoroughly competent professional. Here's what she said:

> *You whom Haggard holds in thrall,*
> *Share his feast and share his fall.*
> *You shall see your fortune flower*
> *Till the torrent takes the tower.*
> *Yet none but one of Hagsgate town*
> *May bring the castle swirling down.*

You'll notice that, like any good curse, this one includes an escape hatch: skip Haggard's feast and you skip the fall, too. Beagle's story doesn't mention anyone who used the escape hatch, but there will have been somebody. There always is; whether we're talking about Númenor, the City of Destruction, the warren of the shining wire, or some other place where a curse is at work, someone's going to walk away. That sounds very heroic in retrospect, but that's not the way it works in practice. In practice, those who walk away are as often as not weeping hysterically, torn between the fear of giving up everything they know and the knowledge that leaving is the only choice left for them, and trying without much success not to listen to the taunts or feel the stones flung by those who stay behind.

If, as Ursula LeGuin says in one of her best stories, they seem to know where they are going, it's because "anywhere but here" is an easy course to chart at first. Mind you, some never even make it out the city gates; some come stumbling back to town a few days or weeks or years later; some are never seen again, and pebbles will grow into moss-covered boulders before anybody finds out exactly what happened to them; still, there's always one, or a few, or nine tall ships sailing from Andunië with stormwinds howling in the rigging, who leave and do something less foredoomed with their lives.

It's the ones who stay behind, though, who are more relevant to the point I want to make. It's very easy to stay behind. Early on, when walking away is an easy thing, the threat of the curse is so far off that it's seductive to think you can stay in Hagsgate for just a little while longer and still escape. Later on, you've come to enjoy the practical benefits that being a citizen of Hagsgate has to offer; you've got personal and financial ties to the place, and so you come up with ornate theories packed with dubious logic and cherrypicked data to convince yourself that the curse isn't real or that it will only affect other people. As the curse begins to work, in turn, you start making excuses, insisting that you did everything you could reasonably be expected to do, and it's all somebody else's fault anyway. Finally, when the full reality of your fate stares you in the face and your last chance of escape is almost gone, comes the terrible temptation to treat the price you're about to pay as a measure of the value of what you've gotten by staying in Hagsgate, and to cling to it ever more frantically as it drags you down.

Now of course a witch didn't actually put a curse on industrial society—at least, if one did, I haven't heard about it—but fairy tales keep their hold on our collective imagination because they contain a wealth of valid wisdom, wrapped up in a compact and memorable form. To say that there's a curse on industrial society is simply to use an archaic metaphor for a point I've been discussing in these essays since *The Archdruid Report* began six years ago, which is that the consequences of industrial society's mismanagement of its relations with the planet will not go away just because we don't want to deal with them. That metaphor has a range of relevant features, and one of them is that any effective response to the curse—or, if you will, the predicament of our time—has to begin by taking stock of the ways that each of us, as individuals, contributes by our own attitudes and actions to the mess we're in, and then making appropriate changes.

After six years, I shouldn't even have to say that daydreaming about running off to some conveniently unaffordable eco-homestead in the country doesn't count. Unless you're in a position to do that, and the vast majority of us aren't, that's simply another evasion. What's required instead is the less romantic but far more productive task of adapting in place: figuring out how, living where you live now, you can place much less of a burden on the biosphere, and help other people do the same thing. It probably has to be said that perfection isn't a reasonable expectation here—there's a long learning curve, and our culture and built environment place significant obstacles in the way—but a great deal can be done nonetheless That can easily lead into activism of various kinds, for those who feel called to do that specific kind of work; it can also lead in plenty of other constructive directions.

Still, that's not a popular message just now, and I'm guessing that it's going to become a great deal more unpopular as industrial civilization stumbles deeper into crisis. It doesn't require a witch's curse to make people cling frantically to exactly those things that are destroying them and their future, just the psychology of previous investment and a few other standard self-defeating habits of the human mind. Still, there's the choice: share the feast and share the fall, or wake up and walk away. Which will you do?

Collapse Now and Avoid the Rush

(Originally published 6 June 2012)

I'm not sure how many people outside the writer's trade realize how much of writing is a cooperative process. That's as true of those of us who write late at night in the privacy of a silent room as it is of the more gregarious sort of writer, the kind you can expect to find in a crowded café, surrounded by voices and music and the clatter of street noises coming in the door: every writer is simply one voice in an ongoing conversation that includes many other voices, some living, some dead and some not yet born.

As I write this week's post, for example, it's difficult not to notice some of the other voices in this particular conversation. The bookshelf an easy reach to my left has a row of brightly colored trade paperbacks by some of my fellow peak oil authors—William Catton, Richard Heinberg, Jim Kunstler, Sharon Astyk, Dmitry Orlov, Carolyn Baker and more. Close by, the rolling brown landscape of Arnold Toynbee's *A Study of History*, all ten volumes, confronts the twin black monoliths of Oswald Spengler's *The Decline of the West*, while Giambattista Vico's *New Science* offers an ironic Italian commentary from one side. Other shelves elsewhere in the room contribute other voices: biology and ecology textbooks from my college days; appropriate tech manuals from the Seventies brimfull of unfulfilled hopes; old texts on the magical philosophy

137

that forms the usually unmentioned foundation from which all my thinking unfolds; and a great deal more. Poets, as often as not, these days: Robinson Jeffers, William Butler Yeats, T.S. Eliot. Without the contributions of all these other voices, the conversation and thus my contributions to it would not be what it is.

Still, there are times when the conversational nature of what I'm doing becomes more obvious and more direct than usual, and one of those happened the weekend before last, at the Age of Limits conference I discussed in last week's post. One of my presentations to that conference was a talk entitled "How Civilizations Fall;" longtime readers of this blog will know from the title that what I was talking about that afternoon was the theory of catabolic collapse, which outlines the way that human societies on the way down cannibalize their own infrastructure, maintaining themselves for the present by denying themselves a future. I finished talking about catabolic collapse and started fielding questions, of which there were plenty, and somewhere in the conversation that followed one of the other participants made a comment. I don't even remember the exact words, but it was something like, "So what you're saying is that what we need to do, individually, is to go through collapse right away."

"Exactly," I said. "Collapse now, and avoid the rush."

Outside of that conversation, I doubt I would have thought of the phrase at all. By the end of the conference, though, it was on the lips of a good many of the attendees, and for good reason: I can't think of a better way to sum up the work ahead of us right now, as industrial society lurches down the far side of its trajectory through time. Longtime readers of this blog know most of the reasoning behind that suggestion, but it may be worth walking through it again step by step.

First, industrial society was only possible because our species briefly had access to an immense supply of cheap, highly concentrated fuel with a very high net energy—that is, the amount of energy needed to extract the fuel was only a very small fraction of the energy the fuel itself provided. Starting in the eighteenth century, fossil fuels—first coal, then coal and petroleum, then coal, petroleum and natural gas—gave us that energy source. All three of these fossil fuels represent millions of years of stored sunlight, captured by the everyday miracle of photosynthesis and concentrated within the earth by geological processes that took place long before our species evolved. They are nonrenewable over any time scale that matters to human beings, and we are using them up at astonishing rates.

Second, while it's easy to suggest that we can simply replace fossil fuels with some other energy source and keep industrial civilization running along its present course, putting that comfortable notion into practice has turned out to be effectively impossible. No other energy source available to our species combines the high net energy, high concentration, and great abundance that a replacement for fossil fuel would need. Those energy sources that are abundant (for example, solar energy) are diffuse and yield little net energy, while those that are highly concentrated (for example, fissionable uranium) are not abundant, and also have serious problems with net energy. Abundant fossil fuels currently provide an "energy subsidy" to alternative energy sources that make them look more efficient than they are—there would be far fewer wind turbines, for example, if they had to be manufactured, installed, and maintained using wind energy. Furthermore, our entire energy infrastructure is geared to use fossil fuels and would have to be replaced, at a cost of countless trillions of dollars, in order to replace fossil fuels with something else.

Third, these problems leave only one viable alternative, which is to decrease our energy use, per capita and absolutely, to get our energy needs down to levels that could be maintained over the long term on renewable sources. The first steps in this process were begun in the 1970s, with good results, and might have made it possible to descend from the extravagant heights of industrialism in a gradual

139

way, keeping a great many of the benefits of the industrial age intact as a gift for the future. Politics closed off that option in the decade that followed, however, and the world's industrial nations went hurtling down a different path, burning through the earth's remaining fossil fuel reserves at an accelerating pace and trusting that economic abstractions such as the free market would suspend the laws of physics and geology for their benefit. At this point, more than three decades after that misguided choice, industrial civilization is so far into overshoot that a controlled descent is no longer an option; the only path remaining is the familiar historical process of decline and fall.

Fourth, while it's fashionable these days to imagine that this process will take the form of a sudden cataclysm that will obliterate today's world overnight, all the testimony of history and a great many lines of evidence from other sources suggests that this is the least likely outcome of our predicament. Across a wide range of geographical scales and technological levels, civilizations take an average of one to three centuries to complete the process of decline and fall, and there is no valid reason to assume that ours will be any exception. The curve of decline, to be sure, is anything but smooth; it has a fractal structure, taking the form of a succession of crises on many different scales, affecting different regions, social classes, and communities in different ways, interspersed with periods of stabilization and even partial recovery that are equally variable in scale, duration, and relevance to different places and groups. This ragged arc of decline is already under way; it can be expected to accelerate in the months, years, and decades to come; and it defines the deindustrial age ahead of us.

Fifth, individuals, families, and communities faced with this predicament still have choices left. The most important of those choices parallels the one faced, or more precisely not faced, at the end of the 1970s: to make the descent in a controlled way, beginning now, or to cling to their current lifestyles until the system that currently supports those lifestyles falls away from beneath their feet. The skills, resources, and lifeways needed to get by in a disintegrating industrial society are radically different from those that made for a successful and comfortable life in the prosperous world of the recent past, and a great many of the requirements of an age of decline come with prolonged learning curves and a high price for failure. Starting right away to practice the skills, assemble the resources, and follow the lifeways that will be the key to survival in a deindustrializing world offers the best hope of getting through the difficult years ahead with some degree of dignity and grace.

Collapse now, in other words, and avoid the rush.

There's a fair amount of subtlety to the strategy defined by those words. As our society stumbles down the ragged curve of its decline, more and more people are going to lose the ability to maintain what counts as a normal lifestyle—or, rather, what counted as a normal lifestyle in the recent past, and is no longer quite so normal today as it once was. Each new round of crisis will push more people further down the slope; minor and localized crises will affect a relatively smaller number of people, while major crises affecting whole nations will affect a much larger number. As each crisis hits, though, there will be a rush of people toward whatever seems to offer a way out, and as each crisis recedes, there will be another rush of people toward whatever seems to offer a way back to what used to be normal. The vast majority of people who join either rush will fail. Remember the tens of thousands of people who applied for a handful of burger-flipping jobs during the recent housing crash, because that was the only job opening they could find? That's the sort of thing I mean.

The way to avoid the rush is simple enough: figure out how you will be able to live after the next wave of crisis hits, and to the extent that you can, *start living that way now*. If you're worried about the long-term prospects for your job—and you probably should be, no matter what you do for a living—now is the time to figure out how you will get by if the job goes away and you have to make do on much less money. For most people, that means getting out of debt, making sure the place you live costs you much less than you can afford, and picking up some practical skills that will allow you to meet some of your own needs and have opportunities for barter and informal employment. It can mean quite a bit more, depending on your situation, needs, and existing skills. It should certainly involve spending less money—and that money, once it isn't needed to pay off any debts you have, can go to weatherizing your home and making other sensible preparations that will make life easier for you later on.

For the vast majority of people, it probably needs to be said, collapsing now does not mean buying a survival homestead somewhere off in the country. That's a popular daydream, and in some well-off circles it's long been a popular way to go have a midlife crisis, but even if you have the funds—and most of us don't—if you don't already have the dizzyingly complex skill set needed to run a viable farm, or aren't willing to drop everything else to apprentice with an organic farmer right now, it's not a realistic option. In all likelihood you'll be experiencing the next round of crises where you are right now, so the logical place to have your own personal collapse now, ahead of the rush, is right there, in the place where you live, with the people you know and the resources you have to hand.

Now of course the strategy of collapsing ahead of the rush is not going to be a popular thing to suggest. When I've brought it up, as of course I've done more than once, I've inevitably fielded a flurry of protests, by turns angry and anguished, insisting that it's not reasonable to expect anybody to do that, and how can I be so heartless as to suggest it? Fair enough; let's take a look at the alternatives.

One alternative strategy that gets brought up now and then has at least the advantage of utter honesty. It has two parts. The first part, while the benefits of industrial society are still available, is to enjoy them; the second, when those benefits go away, is to die. Often, though not always, the people who bring up this option have serious health conditions that will probably be fatal in a deindustrial world. I have no quarrel with those who choose this path; it's an honest response to a very challenging predicament—though I admit I wonder how many people who say they've chosen it will be comfortable with their choice once part one gives way to part two.

The problem with the other proposed strategies for dealing with our predicament is that whatever they claim to do in theory, in practice, they amount to these same two steps. Consider the very widely held notion that advocating for some alternative energy technology is a workable response to the twilight of fossil fuels. I have no quarrel, again, with people who are actually doing something concrete to get some alternative energy technology into use—for example, the people whose enthusiasm for the Bussard fusion reactor leads them to build a prototype in their basement, or to help fund one of the half dozen or so experimenters who have already done this—but that's rarely what this approach entails; rather, it seems to consist mostly of posting long screeds on the internet insisting that thorium reactors, or algal biodiesel, or what have you, will solve all our energy problems.

As Zen masters like to say, talk does not cook the rice, and blog posts do not build reactors; with every day that passes, despite any amount of online debate, more oil, coal, and natural gas are extracted from the planet's dwindling endowment, and the next round of crises comes closer. In the same way, those who put their hopes on grand political transformations, or conveniently undefinable leaps of consciousness, or the timely arrival of Jesus or the space brothers or somebody else who will spare us the necessity of inhabiting a future that is the exact result of our own collective actions, are not doing anything that hasn't been tried over and over again in the decades just past, without doing anything to slow the headless rush into overshoot or the opening stages of decline and fall.

Check out the glossy magazines and well-funded websites dedicated to portraying "positive futures" and you can find the same sort of thinking taken to its logical extreme: soothing pablum about this or that person doing this or that wonderful thing, and this or that deep thinker coming up with this or that wonderful idea, all of it reminiscent of nothing so much as the cheerful tunes the *Titanic's* band played to keep the passengers calm as water poured into the hull. There's quite a lot of money to be made these days insisting that we can have a shiny new future despite all evidence to the contrary, and pulling factoids out of context to defend that increasingly dubious claim; as industrial society moves down the curve of decline, I suspect, this will become even more popular, since it will make it easier for those who haven't yet had their own personal collapse to pretend that it can't happen to them.

The same principle applies to the people who donate to environmental causes and put solar panels on their roofs in the same spirit that led medieval Christians to buy high-priced indulgences from the Church to cancel out their sins. T.S. Eliot countered that sort of attitude unanswerably when he described salvation as "a condition of complete simplicity, costing not less than everything."[*] What we're discussing belongs to a much less exalted plane, but the same rule applies: if you're trying to exempt yourself from the end of the industrial age, nothing you can do can ever be enough. Let go, let yourself fall forward into the deindustrial future, and matters are different.

It's difficult to think of anything more frightening, or more necessary. "In order to arrive at what you do not know"—that's Eliot again—"you must go by a way which is the way of ignorance. In order to possess what you do not possess, you must go by the way of dispossession." Which is to say: collapse now, and avoid the rush.

---

[*] This quotation is from "Little Gidding," and the following one from "East Coker," both in *Four Quartets* (Harcourt Brace Jovanovich, 1971).

Parting of the Ways

(Originally published 13 June 2012)

Chalk it up to an adolescence spent reading such cheerful books as *The Limits to Growth* and *The Coming Dark Age*, but it takes quite a bit to make me fret about the future. Even now, as industrial civilization begins to sink down the far side of Hubbert's curve, and facts and figures come rolling in on a daily basis to sketch the predicament of our time in ever more detail, I usually find it easy to nod and make a note and go on with the work at hand, whether that's bringing in greens and snow peas from the garden or hammering out this week's *Archdruid Report* post.

Still, a series of news items over the last week or so have me worried. No, it's not the latest news about methane plumes in the Arctic Ocean; it's not the current round of economic idiocy from Europe, where the bizarre conviction that banks ought to be sheltered from the consequences of even their most clueless investment decisions has become the centerpiece of an economic nonpolicy that will likely tip the entire EU into mass bankruptcy; it's not the death struggle between two failed ideologies that's frozen Washington DC into utter political paralysis at a time when avoiding hard questions any longer may well put the survival of the nation at risk. No, quite the contrary: it's the rising chorus of voices, from all across the political and cultural spectrum, insisting that everything really is all right and that any suggestion to the contrary ought to be shouted down as quickly as possible.

That's been one of the less useful habits of large parts of the American right for some time now. Still, the habit of detachment from reality reached new lows this month, as North Carolina's senate passed legislation forbidding the state from considering scientific evidence for rising sea levels in any policy dealing with the state's low and vulnerable coastline. Texas and Virginia have already taken similar steps; it's reminiscent of King Canute, who famously commanded the tide to retreat and just as famously got his royal feet good and wet. Since all three of these states are in the hurricane belt, and rising sea levels add mightily to the destructive impact of hurricane storm surges, it's unlikely that this attempt to better Canute's score will end so harmlessly.

Over on the other side of the spectrum, mind you, there's no shortage of equivalent ideas. My fellow peak oil blogger Jan Lundberg, an activist well over on the leftward side of things, recently posted a thoughtful critique[*] of the ideas on display at a San Francisco alternative culture expo. In there with the alternative healers and pop mysticism was a pervasive and contemptuous rejection of the idea that there might be limits to material abundance. That habit's been popular in the New Age scene for decades—Rhonda Byrne's meretricious *The Secret*, with its insistence that focusing on your sense of personal entitlement will browbeat the universe into giving you all the goodies you want, has a long pedigree—but as Lundberg pointed out, it's become tangled up with frankly paranoid conspiracy theories and frankly delusional notions about the human mind's alleged ability to repeal the laws of thermodynamics. Lundberg suggests that what's emerging here is a New Age equivalent to the Tea Party, and he's quite correct: there's really not much to choose between "visualize, baby, visualize" and "drill, baby, drill."

I had a personal run-in with the same sort of thinking not long ago, in the course of finding a publisher for *After Oil*, the anthology of peak oil science fiction to which this blog's readers contributed so

---

[*] http://www.culturechange.org/cms/content/view/841/1

many excellent stories late last year. (Yes, it's going to press; I hope to have a tentative release date shortly.) One potential publisher, who had been enthusiastic about the project early on, rejected it with some heat once he read the manuscript. He didn't object to the literary quality of the stories; no, what upset him was the fact that the stories assumed that people in a post-peak oil world would be more or less like people today, living in a world no more loaded with miracles than the one we now inhabit. Why, he asked, couldn't the authors have written stories in which the problem of peak oil was solved by people sprouting psychic antennae, or creating new forms of kinship with water molecules, or at the very least powering the world on algae fuel?

Now of course there is an answer to that question, which is that the point of the anthology was to tell stories about the kind of futures we're going to get, rather than chasing pretty daydreams that start by pretending that the realities of our predicament don't apply to us. In the real world, my readers will have noticed, there's a distinct shortage of people who grow antennae, psychic or otherwise; while cultivating a sense of kinship with water molecules seems reasonable enough to me—the human body is mostly water, after all—it's not going to make water behave any differently than it does today; and there are solid thermodynamic reasons, discussed here and elsewhere, why algal biodiesel will never be more than a laboratory curiosity on the one hand, and a lure for unwary investors on the other. Still, it became clear very quickly that this answer was not the sort of thing the publisher wanted to hear.

It's something a great many people don't want to hear these days, and the refusal to hear it is getting distinctly shrill in some quarters— consider the angry tone of the latest press releases from the financial sphere insisting that peak oil is nonsense—after all, it ought to be obvious to any reasonable person that waving around enough money will brush aside the laws of physics and geology, right? Not too long ago, that insistence used to be expressed in tones of insufferable superiority—think of Daniel Yergin's dismissals of peak oil, or the airy optimism of Bjorn Lomborg's *The Skeptical Environmentalist*. Now of course Lomborg insisted that the price of oil would remain at $20 to $30 a barrel through 2020, and Yergin in 2004 claimed that the price of oil had reached a permanent plateau at $38 a barrel; the failure of oil prices to do as they were told doubtless contributed to the more strident tone such proclamations so often get these days.

Still, it's not the shrill tone of the latest round that has me watching with more than the usual concern. It's the increasing sense that not even the people who are promoting such claims actually believe them any more. The North Carolina legislators who are trying to pretend that sea level rise won't happen, like their equivalents in Texas and Virginia, remind me of nothing so much as six-year-olds who stuff their fingers in their ears, scrunch their eyes shut, and chant "I can't hear you, la la la" at the top of their lungs. The New Age equivalent is a little more subtle, but after half a century of failed predictions of saucer landings and leaps of consciousness—and let's not even talk about what happened to the millions of Americans who tried to use *The Secret* to make boatloads of money for nothing by investing in the late real estate bubble—there can't be many people left in the scene who don't know, on some level, that they're kidding themselves. For that matter, if the publisher who turned down *After Oil* suddenly sprouted a pair of antennae, it's probably a safe bet that, instead of embracing the event as a welcome miracle, he'd call a dermatologist in a fair state of panic.

If that's the case—if the incantations being repeated these days to justify doing nothing significant about the crisis of our age are no longer even plausible to most of the people who mouth them—we are a good deal closer to a critical juncture in the downward slide than I thought. Visible ahead of us is a parting of the ways that will define a great deal of what we will experience in the years to come.

To understand that parting of the ways, it's important to get a good clear sense of how self-deception works. I suspect most of my readers have had the experience of arguing themselves into believing, at least for a short time, something that they knew was not true. It's a fascinating study in the corruption of the intellect. To start with, much more often than not, questions of the truth of the belief in question are ignored or actively evaded; what matters is that accepting the false belief will bring practical benefits, or please another person, or identify the believer with an admirable person or group.

As the false belief is affirmed in public and expressed in action, though, the critical space required to accept the belief publicly without believing it inwardly trickles away. The cognitive dissonance that comes from affirming and enacting a belief without believing it is hard to bear, and the more the belief is affirmed and enacted, the more painful the dissonance becomes. One way out of the dissonance is to abandon the false belief, but social pressures often make that a costly and embarrassing step; the other option, to make yourself believe that the false belief is true, routinely comes with equally substantial social rewards. It's not surprising that a significant number of people make that latter choice.

Once it's made, though, the pathologies of repressed disbelief unfold in predictable ways. The believer becomes brittle and defensive about the false belief, affirming it loudly and publicly, and taking on the familiar social role of the strident true believer. Elaborate arguments for the truth of the false belief take on an ever larger role in his mental life; if books of such arguments exist, you can count on finding them on his bookshelves, while his willingness to encounter differing views—not even opposing ones, but simply those that are not identical to the cherished false belief—drops like a rock.

Convincing the rest of the world of the truth of the false belief becomes a central concern, since every new convert to the false belief helps shore up the believer's self-imposed conviction that the false belief really is true. Onto those who refuse to be converted, meanwhile, the believer projects not only his own unspoken doubts, but the bad faith and hypocrisy that surrounds those doubts. Thus, in the mind of the believer, the unbeliever gets turned into a caricature of everything the believer can't stand in himself, and serves by turns as a straw man, a scapegoat, and the supposed cause of everything evil in the world.

How this trajectory ends is determined by the nature of the false belief itself, or more precisely by the relation between the false belief and the world of objective fact. If the belief does not require the world to behave in a way that it manifestly doesn't, it's entirely possible for believers to spend the rest of their lives loudly proclaiming the truth of a belief they know is false, and hating those people who reject the belief for openly speaking the truth the believers are unwilling to utter, without going further into oughtright psychopathology. It's when the false belief makes specific, falsifiable claims about the way the world works that problems crop up; the more central these claims are to the belief system, and the more obviously and repeatedly the claims are falsified, the more difficult those problems become.

The most productive way to cope with those problems is to abandon the false belief, and of course a good many people do that after a sufficiently forceful disconfirmation. Much less productive is the option of doubling down on the belief system, insisting on its truth in the face of any amount of evidence, and following it out to its logical conclusions no matter how horrific those happen to be. That's how mass suicides happen: back yourself into the blind alley of unconditional commitment to a belief you know to be false, and reject even the slightest doubt about the belief as a failure that's unthinkable precisely because you're constantly thinking it, and the temptation to prove your loyalty to the false belief in the one ultimately unanswerable way can be very hard to resist.

Most of my readers will be able to call examples of this trajectory easily to mind, and a fair number will have experienced at least a small part of it themselves. I've come to think, though, that in the years immediately ahead of us, it's going to be almost possible to miss. Plenty of belief systems will have to deal with repeated disconfirmation, but the one that's likely to get hit the hardest, and may well produce the biggest crop of pathological behavior, is the established religion of the modern industrial world, the belief in the inevitability and goodness of progress.

I'd like to suggest that it's precisely the failure of the modern faith in progress that's driving the rush to illusion discussed earlier in this post. Belief in progress has no place for the awkward reality that the wastes we're pumping into the atmosphere are putting pressure on an already unstable global climate, sending meltwater flooding into the oceans and raising sea level; after all, according to the believers, progress is supposed to solve problems, not cause them. Belief in progress has no place for the hard fact that economic abundance can't simply be wished into being, but depends on ample supplies of the cheap, concentrated energy that, in this corner of the universe, can only be had in sufficient quantities from the fossil fuels we're depleting so rapidly. Belief in progress has no place at all, finally, for the unwelcome but necessary recognition that we won't get far by sitting on our backsides and waiting for psychic antennae or some other miracle to save us from the consequences of our own mistakes.

Precisely because it has no place for these things, in turn, the faith in progress is taking quite a beating these days. As the United States quietly folds up its space program, hands over its infrastructure to malign neglect, allows measures of public health to drop toward Third World levels, and lets what's left of its economy devolves into a dishonest casino game, the mere fact that a narrowing circle of well-off individuals can buy electronic toys slightly more complex than last year's equivalents just doesn't have the cachet it once did. Even the mainstream media has had a harder time clinging to the mythic power of progress than it once did; it's symptomatic that the Wall Street Journal's MarketWatch—reread that, and let it sink in for a moment—recently hosted an essay[*] pointing out that the idea of infinite growth is a delusion, and that economics has become a pseudoscience

---

[*] www.marketwatch.com/story/myth-of-perpetual-growth-is-killing-america-2012-06-12

incapable of providing meaningful information about the future. ("What do you call an economist who makes a prediction? Wrong.")

The question is how people will react to the increasing disconfirmation of the myth of progress. Some, I am relieved to say, have bitten the bullet, accepted the fact that progress was a temporary condition made possible by extravagant and unsustainable exploitation of the Earth's fossil fuel reserves, and begun to grapple with the challenges and possibilities of a future where progress no longer takes place and contraction and regression are the rule. More will likely do so as we proceed—many more, in all probability, than I thought possible when I launched this blog six years ago. Still, I doubt the refusal to give up on the failed myth will be limited to North Carolina politicians, San Francisco New Age aficionados, and avant-garde publishers.

I suspect, rather, that the refusal to recognize and deal with the end of progress will become a massive social force in the decade or so ahead of us, and that the great divide in American society during those years will not be the one between left and right, or between rich and poor, but between those who have accepted history's verdict on our fantasy of perpetual progress, on the one hand, and those who cling to the fantasy despite all disconfirmations, on the other. Since refusing to recognize the fact of decline is a good way to get clobbered over the head by one or another of that fact's manifestations—a point that the inhabitants of coastal North Carolina are likely to find out the hard way one of these days—those who choose the path of denial may be in for a very rough road indeed.

The Upside of Default

(Originally published 25 July 2012)

Writing *The Archdruid Report* has its pleasures, and one of them is the wry amusement to be had when some caustic jab of mine turns into an accurate prediction of the future. Longtime readers may recall a comment of mine late last year to the effect that ordinary investors would surely find some way to pile into the shale gas bubble before the next year was out. Thanks to an anonymous reader and the August 2012 edition of *SmartMoney* Magazine, which arrived from said reader in yesterday's mail, that comment can now be moved over into the "confirmed" category.

The prediction, to be sure, didn't require any particular clairvoyance on my part. Its sources are, first, a decent grasp of the history of economic stupidity, and second, a keen sense of the levels of desperation in what we might as well call the investmentariat, the people who have a little money and are looking for a safe place to put it. The investmentariat has been told for decades that their money ought to make them money, but nobody told them that this only works in an economy that experiences sustained real growth over the long term, and nobody would dream of mentioning in their hearing that we don't have an economy like that anymore.

All the investmentariat knows for sure is that the kind of safe investment that used to bring in five per cent a year is now yielding a small fraction of one per cent, and the risks you need to take to get five per cent a year are those once associated with the the kind of "securities" that make a mockery of that title. The resulting panic is *SmartMoney*'s bread and butter. Smart money in the old sense—that is to say, the people who know what's going on in the sordid and scam-ridden world of investment—wouldn't waste five seconds on such a magazine; they know you can't get any kind of advantage from something that a couple of million people are also reading. No, this is strictly for the investmentariat: as glossy, glib, and superficial as a teen fashion magazine, and just as unerringly aimed at the lowest common denominator of contemporary thought.

It will thus come as no surprise that the cover story on the August 2012 issue of *SmartMoney* is "The Return of Fossil Fuels," and that it rehashes the latest clichés about vast new gas and oil reserves without asking any of the the inconvenient questions that a competent practitioner of the lost art of journalism, should one be wakened from enchanted sleep by the touch of a 1940s radio microphone, would ask as a matter of course. The article trumpets the fact that America is importing less oil than last year, for example, without mentioning that this is because Americans are using less oil—unemployed people who've exhausted their 99 weeks of benefits don't take many Sunday drives—and it babbles about natural gas for two largely fact-free pages without mentioning that claims about vast supplies far into the future rely on assumptions about the production decline rate from fracked shale gas wells that make professionals in the gas drilling industry snort beer out their noses.

All this, inevitably, is window dressing for suggestions about which stocks you should buy so you can cash in on the fracking boom. Last I heard, it was still illegal for journalists to take payola for pimping individual companies, or to speculate in the stocks they promote; still, I trust my readers will already have realized that one set of professional market players will get copies of the magazine the moment it hits the newsstand, snap up shares in the companies promoted in each issue, and dole them out at inflated prices to

SmartMoney readers who get their magazines later, while another set of professional market players will take out short contracts on those same stocks as they peak, wait for the rush of buyers to crest and recede, and cash in on the inevitable losses. Those are among the ways the game is played—and if this suggests to you, dear reader, that the readers of *SmartMoney* are not going to get rich from shale gas by following this month's tips, well, yes, that's what it means.

This is business as usual in the financial industry, which has made a lucrative business out of extracting wealth from the investmentariat in various ways. This is part and parcel of the broader and even more lucrative business of extracting wealth from everywhere by every available means. The question that might be worth asking here, and is rarely asked anywhere, is whether the financial industry provides anything to the rest of the economy commensurate with its immense income and profits. Any economics textbook will tell you that companies raise capital by issuing stock, selling bonds, and engaging in a few other kinds of transactions in the financial markets, and that this plays a crucial role in enabling economic growth. Well and good; there are many other ways to do the same thing, but we'll accept that this is the way modern industrial societies allot capital to new and expanding businesses. How much of the financial industry's total paper value has anything to do with this service?

Let's do some back of the envelope calculations. In 2010, the latest year for which I could find figures, the total value of bonds issued by nonfinancial businesses was $1.3 trillion, and the total net issuance of stock by all companies was $387 billion—that includes stock issued by financial businesses, but since this is a rough estimate we'll let that pass. Total stock and bond issuance in 2010 to support the production of real goods and services was thus something less than $1.7 trillion; let's double that figure, just to leave adequate room for other ways of raising capital that might otherwise slip through the cracks, for a very rough order-ofmagnitude figure around $3.4 trillion.

In 2010, the total stock of debt and equity potentially available for trading in financial markets was $212 trillion, and the total notional value of derivatives that same year was estimated at $707 trillion. Exactly how much of this was traded in the course of the year on all markets is anybody's guess—some stocks heavily traded by computer programs may change hands dozens of times in a day, while other assets spent the whole year sitting in a safe deposit box; still, this is back-of-the-envelope stuff, so we'll use the total value just listed as a very rough measure of the size of the financial economy. We can round up a little here, too, to make room for forms of wealth not included in the two categories just named, and estimate the total paper value of the world's financial wealth at $1 quadrillion, of which the fraction directed into the productive economy in one year amounts to around a third of one per cent.

Now of course providing capital to the productive economy is only one of the things the financial industry does that's arguably useful to someone other than financiers. Local and national governments use the financial industry to raise funds for public works, individuals borrow money for the occasional useful purpose, and so on. Let's be generous, and assume that the amount of money that flows from the world of finance for these purposes is double the total input of capital into nonfinancial businesses via stocks and bonds. That means that in any given year, maybe one per cent of the financial economy has anything to do with the production of real, nonfinancial goods and services.

The rest? It consists of ways to make money from money. That seems innocuous enough, until you remember what money actually is. Money is not wealth; it's a system of abstract, culturally contrived tokens that we use to manage the distribution of real goods and services. A money system can simplify the process of putting energy, raw materials, labor, and other goods and services to work in productive ways; that's the reason we have money, or rather the reason most of us are prepared to discuss in public. That's not what the other 99% of the world's financial assets are doing, though. They are there to ensure that the people who own them have disproportionate, unearned access to real, nonfinancial goods and services. That's the other reason, the one nobody wants to mention.

Not that many centuries ago, across much of the world, usury—lending money at interest—was considered a serious crime, more serious than robbery, and was also classed as a mortal sin by Christian and Muslim religious authorities; it's no accident that Dante consigned usurers to the lowest pit of the seventh circle of Hell. That's been dismissed as a bit of primitive moralizing by modern writers, but that dismissal is yet another example of the way that contemporary industrial culture has ignored the painfully learned lessons of the past. In a steady-state or contracting economy, usury is a parasite that kills its host; since the total stock of real wealth does not expand from one year to the next, each interest payment enriches the lender but leaves the borrower permanently poorer.

Only in an expanding economy can usury be tolerated, since interest can be paid out of the proceeds of economic growth. Periods of sustained economic expansion are rare in human history, since most societies live close to the edge of the limits to growth in their bioregions; the exceptions, such as the late Roman Republic and early Empire, usually involve the expansion of one society at the expense of others. The late Roman Republic and early Empire, it may be worth noting, had a large and very successful moneylending industry, which fed on the expanding Roman state in much the same way that the Roman state fed on the accumulated wealth of the Mediterranean world. Only after Roman expansion stopped did attitudes shift, in favor of a religion that was violently opposed to usury.

During the three centuries of their power, the world's industrial nations looted their nonindustrial neighbors with as much enthusiasm as the ancient Romans looted theirs, but they had another source of plunder—half a billion years of fossil sunlight, stored up in the form of coal, oil, and natural gas. In effect, we stripped prehistory to the bare walls so that we could enjoy an age of gargantuan excess unlike any other. One consequence was that our moneylending industry was able to metastasize to a scale no previous gang of usurers has ever been able to attain. The basic arithmetic remains unchanged, though: usury is only viable in an expanding economy, and as the global economy enters its post-peak oil decline, the entire structure of money that makes money, is going to come apart at the seams.

I'd like to suggest, in fact, that the unspoken subtext behind the financial crises of recent years is precisely that the real economy of goods and services is no longer growing enough to support the immense financial economy that parasitizes it. The current crisis in Europe is a case in point. Since the crisis dawned in 2008, EU policy has demanded that every other sector of the economy be thrown under the bus in order to prop up the tottering mass of unpayable debt that Europe's financial economy has become. As banks fail, governments have been strongarmed into guaranteeing the value of the banks' worthless financial paper; as governments fail in their turn, other governments that are still solvent are being pressured to fill the gap with bailouts that, again, amount to little more than a guarantee that even the most harebrained investment will not be allowed to lose money.

The problem, as the back of the envelope calculations above might suggest, is that you can cash in the whole planet's gross domestic product—that was a little under $62 trillion in 2010—and not come anywhere close to the value of the mountain of increasingly fictive paper wealth that's been piled up by the financial industry in the last few decades. Thus the EU's strategy is guaranteed to fail. EU officials are already talking about "haircuts" for bondholders—that's financial jargon for investors not getting paid as much as their holdings are theoretically worth. Not so long ago, that possibility was unmentionable; now it's being embraced frantically as the only alternative to what's actually going to happen, which is default.

There's been a lot of talk about that in the blogosphere of late, and for good reason. No matter how you twist and turn the matter, Greece is never going to be able to pay its national debt. Neither are Spain, Italy, or half a dozen other nations that ran up big debts when it was cheap and convenient to do so, and are now being strangled by a panicking bond market and a collapsing economy. This isn't new; most of the countries on Earth have either defaulted outright on their debts or forced renegotiations on their creditors that left the latter with some equivalent of pennies on the dollar. The US last did that in a big way in 1934, when the Roosevelt administration unilaterally changed the terms on billions of dollars in Liberty Bonds from "payable in gold" to "payable in devalued dollars," and proceeded to print the latter as needed. That or considerably worse will be happening in Europe in the near future, too.

A good deal of the discussion of these upcoming defaults in the blogosphere, though, has insisted that these defaults will lead to a complete collapse of the world's financial economy, and from there to an equally complete collapse of the world's productive economy, leaving all seven billion of us to starve in the gutter. It's an odd belief, since sovereign debt defaults have happened many times in the recent past, currency collapses are far from rare in economic history, and nation-states can do—and have done—plenty of drastic things to keep goods and services flowing in an economic emergency. Partly, I suspect, it's our old friend the apocalypse meme—the notion, pervasive in modern culture, that the only alternative to the indefinite continuation of business as usual is some unparalleled cataclysm or other.

Still, there's another dimension to these fantasies, which is simply that the financial industry has done a superb job of convincing people that what they do is important to the rest of us. It's true, to be sure, that having currency in circulation makes economic exchanges easier, and the kind of banking services that people and ordinary businesses use are also very helpful, but governments used to produce and circulate currency without benefit of banks until fairly recently, and banking services of the kind I've just mentioned can be provided quickly and easily by a government that means business; in 1933 it took the US government just over a week, at a time when information technology was incomparably slower than it is today, to nationalize every bank in the country and open their doors under Federal management. The other services the financial industry provides to the real economy can equally well be replaced by hastily kluged substitutes, or simply put on hold for the duration of the crisis.

So the downside of any financial crisis, however grandiose, can be stopped promptly by proven methods. Then there's the upside. Yes, there's an upside. That's the ultimate secret of the financial crisis, the thing that nobody anywhere wants to talk about: if a country gets into a credit crisis, defaulting on its debts is the one option that consistently leads to recovery.

That statement ought to be old hat by now. Russia defaulted on its debts in 1998, and that default marked the end of its post-Soviet economic crisis and the beginning of its current period of relative prosperity. Argentina defaulted on its debts in 2002, and the default put an end to its deep recession and set it on the road to recovery. Even more to the point, Iceland was the one European country that refused the EU demand that the debts of failed banks must be passed on to governments; instead, in 2008, the Icelandic government allowed the country's three biggest banks to fold, paid off Icelandic depositors by way of the existing deposit insurance scheme, and left foreign investors twisting in the wind. Since that time, Iceland has been the only European country to see a sustained recovery.

When Greece defaults on its debts and leaves the Euro, in turn, there will be a bit of scrambling, and then the Greek recovery will begin. That's the reason the EU has been trying so frantically to keep Greece from defaulting, no matter how many Euros have to be shoveled down how many ratholes to prevent it. Once the Greek default happens, and it will—the number of ratholes is multiplying much faster than Euros can be shoveled into them—the other southern European nations that are crushed by excessive debt will line up to do the same. There will be a massive stock market crash, a great many banks will go broke, a lot of rich people and an even larger number of middle class people will lose a great deal of money, politicians will make an assortment of stern and defiant speeches, and then the great European financial crisis will be over and people can get on with their lives.

That's what will happen, too, another five or ten or fifteen years down the road, when the United States either defaults on its national debt or hyperinflates the debt out of existence. It's going to do one or the other, since its debts are already unpayable except by way of the printing press, and its gridlocked political system is unable either to rationalize its tax system or cut its expenditures. The question is simply what crisis will finally break the confidence of foreign investors in the dollar as a safe haven currency, and start the panic selling of dollar-denominated assets that will tip the US into its next really spectacular financial crisis. That's going to be a messy one, since the financial economy is so deeply woven into the fantasy life of the average American; there will be a lot of poverty and suffering, as there always is during serious financial crises, but as John Kenneth Galbraith pointed out about an earlier crisis of the same kind, "while it is a time of great tragedy, nothing is being lost but money."[*]

It will be after that, in turn, that the next round of temporary recovery can begin. We'll talk more about that in the weeks to come.

---

[*]   J.K. Galbraith, *The Great Crash 1929* (New York: Houghton & Mifflin, 1961), p. 2.

The Beginning of the World

(Originally published 26 December 2012)

Last Friday was, as I'm sure most of my readers noticed, an ordinary day. Here in the north central Appalachians, it was chilly but not unseasonably so, with high gray clouds overhead and a lively wind setting the dead leaves aswirl; wrens and sparrows hopped here and there in my garden, poking among the recently turned soil of the beds. No cataclysmic earth changes, alien landings, returning messiahs, or vast leaps of consciousness disturbed their foraging. They neither knew nor cared that one of the great apocalyptic delusions of modern times was reaching its inevitable end around them.

The inimitable Dr. Rita Louise, on whose radio talk show I spent a couple of hours on Friday, may have summed it up best when she wished her listeners a happy Mayan Fools Day. Not that the ancient Mayans themselves were fools, far from it, but then they had precisely nothing to do with the competing fantasies of doom and universal enlightenment that spent the last decade and more buzzing like flies around last Friday's date.

It's worth taking a look back over the genesis of the 2012 hysteria, if only because we're certain to see plenty of reruns in the years ahead. In the first half of the twentieth century, as archeologists learned to read dates in the Mayan Long Count calendar, it became clear that one of the major cycles of the old Mayan timekeeping system would roll over on that day. By the

1970s, that detail found its way into alternative culture in the United States, setting off the first tentative speculations about a 2012 apocalypse, notably drug guru Terence McKenna's quirky "Timewave Zero" theory.

It was the late New Age promoter Jose Arguelles, though, who launched the 2012 fad on its way with his 1984 book *The Mayan Factor* and a series of sequels, proclaiming that the rollover of the Mayan calendar in 2012 marked the imminent transformation of human consciousness that the New Age movement was predicting so enthusiastically back then. The exactness of the date made an intriguing contrast with the vagueness of Arguelles' predictions about it, and this contrast left ample room for other authors in the same field to jump on the bandwagon and redefine the prophecy to fit whatever their own eschatological preferences happened to be. This they promptly did.

Early on, 2012 faced plenty of competition from alternative dates for the great transformation. The year 2000 had been a great favorite for a century, and became 2012's most important rival, but it came and went without bringing anything more interesting than another round of sordid business as usual. Thereafter, 2012 reigned supreme, and became the center of a frenzy of anticipation that was at least as much about marketing as anything else. I can testify from my own experience that for a while there, late in the last decade, if you wanted to write a book about anything even vaguely tangential to New Age subjects and couldn't give it a 2012 spin, many publishers simply weren't interested.

So the predictions piled up. The fact that no two of them predicted the same thing did nothing to weaken the mass appeal of the date. Neither did the fact, which became increasingly clear as the last months of 2012 approached, that a great many people who talked endlessly about the wonderful or terrible things that were about to happen weren't acting as though they believed a word of it. That was by and large as true of the New Age writers and pundits who fed the hysteria as it was of their readers and audiences; I long ago lost track of the number of 2012 prophets who, aside from scheduling a holiday trip to the Yucatan or some other fashionable spot for the big day, acted in all respects as though they expected the world to keep going in its current manner straight into 2013 and beyond.

That came as a surprise to me. Regular readers may recall my earlier speculation that 2012 would see scenes reminiscent of the "Great Disappointment" of 1844, with crowds of true believers standing on hilltops waiting for their first glimpse of alien spacecraft descending from heaven or what have you. Instead, in the last months of this year, some of the writers and pundits most deeply involved in the 2012 hysteria started claiming that, well, actually, December 21st wasn't going to be the day everything changed; it would, ahem, usher in a period of transition of undefined length during which everything would sooner or later get around to changing. The closer last Friday came, the more evasive the predictions became, and Mayan Fools Day and its aftermath were notable for the near-total silence that spread across the apocalyptic end of the blogosphere. Say what you will about Harold Camping, at least he had the courage to go on the air after his May prophecy flopped and admit that he must have gotten his math wrong somewhere.

Now of course Camping went on at once to propose a new date for the Rapture, which flopped with equal inevitability a few months later. It's a foregone conclusion that some of the 2012 prophets will do the same thing shortly, if only to kick the apocalypse marketing machine back into gear. It's entirely possible that they'll succeed in setting off a new frenzy for some other date, because the social forces that make apocalyptic fantasies so tempting to believe just now have not lost any of their potency.

The most important of those forces, as I've argued in previous posts, is the widening mismatch between the fantasy of entitlement that has metastasized through contemporary American society, on the one hand, and the ending of an age of fossil-fueled imperial extravagance on the other. As the United States goes bankrupt trying to maintain its global empire, and industrial civilization as a whole slides down the far side of a dizzying range of depletion curves, it's becoming harder by the day for Americans to make believe that the old saws of upward mobility and an ever brighter future have any relevance to their own lives—and yet those beliefs are central to the psychology, the self-image, and the worldview of most Americans. The resulting cognitive dissonance is hard to bear, and apocalyptic fantasies offer a convenient way out. They promise that the world will change, so that the believers don't have to.

That same frantic desire to ignore the arrival of inescapable change pervades today's cultural scene, even in those subcultures that insist most loudly that change is what they want. In recent months, to cite only one example, nearly every person who's mentioned to me the claim that climate change could make the Earth uninhabitable has gone on to ask, often in so many words, "So why should I consume less now?" The overt logic here is usually that individual action can't possibly be enough. Whether or not that's true is anyone's guess, but cutting your own carbon footprint actually does *something*, which is more than can be said for sitting around enjoying a standard industrial world lifestyle while waiting for that imaginary Kum Ba Ya moment when everyone else in the world will embrace limits not even the most ardent climate change activists are willing to accept themselves.

Another example? Consider the rhetoric of elite privilege that clusters around the otherwise inoffensive label "1%." That rhetoric plays plenty of roles in today's society, but one of them pops up reliably any time I talk about using less. Why, people ask me in angry tones, should they give up their cars when the absurdly rich are enjoying gigantic luxury yachts? Now of course we could have a conversation about the total contribution to global warming of cars owned by people who aren't rich, compared to that of the fairly small number of top-end luxury yachts that usually figure in such arguments, but there's another point that needs to be raised. None of the people who make this argument to me have any control over whether rich people have luxury yachts. All of them have a great deal of control over whether and how often they themselves use cars. Blaming the global ecological crisis on the very rich thus functions, in practice, as one more way to evade the necessity of unwelcome change.

Along these same lines, dear reader, as you surf the peak oil and climate change blogosphere and read the various opinions on display there, I'd encourage you to ask yourself what those opinions amount to in actual practice. A remarkably large fraction of them, straight across the political landscape from furthest left to furthest right and including all stops in between, add up to demands that somebody else, somewhere else, do something. Since the people making such demands rarely do anything to pressure, or even to encourage, those other people elsewhere to do whatever it is they're supposed to do, it's not exactly hard to do the math and recognize that here again, these opinions amount to so many ways of insisting that the people holding them don't have to give up the extravagant and unsustainable lifestyles most people in the industrial world think of as normal and justifiable.

There's another way to make the same point, which is that most of what you'll see being proposed in the peak oil and climate change blogosphere has been proposed over and over and over again already, without the least impact on our predicament. From the protest marches and the petitions, through the latest round of grand plans for energy futures destined to sit on the shelves cheek by jowl with the last round, right up to this week's flurry of buoyantly optimistic blog posts lauding any technofix you care to name from cold fusion and algal biodiesel to shale gas and drill-baby-drill: been there, done that, used the T-shirt to wipe another dozen endangered species off the face of the planet, and we're still stuck in the same place. The one thing next to nobody wants to talk about is the one thing that distinguished the largely successful environmental movement of the 1960s and 1970s from the largely futile environmental movement since that time, which is that activists in the earlier movement were willing to start the ball rolling by making the necessary changes in their own lives first.

The difficulty, of course, is that making these changes is precisely what many of today's green activists are desperately trying to avoid. That's understandable, since transitioning to a lifestyle that's actually sustainable involves giving up many of the comforts, perks, and privileges central to the psychology and identity of people in modern industrial societies. In today's world of accelerating downward mobility, especially, the thought of taking any action that might result in being mistaken for the poor is something most Americans in particular can't bear to contemplate—even when those same Americans recognize on some level that sooner or later, like it or not, they're going to end up poor anyway.

Those of my readers who would like to see this last bit of irony focused to incandescence need only get some comfortably middle class eco-liberal to start waxing lyrical about life in the sustainable world of the future, when we'll all have to get by on a small fraction of our current resource base. This is rarely difficult; I field such comments quite often, sketching out a rose-colored contrast between today's comfortable but unsatisfying lifestyles and the more meaningful and fulfilling existence that will be ours in a future of honest hard work in harmony with nature. Wait until your target is in full spate, and then point out that he could embrace that more meaningful and fulfilling lifestyle right now by the simple expedient of discarding the comforts and privileges that stand in the way. You'll get to watch backpedaling on a heroic scale, accompanied by a flurry of excuses meant to justify your target's continued dependence on the very comforts and privileges he was belittling a few moments before.

What makes the irony perfect is that, by and large, the people whom you'll hear criticizing the modern lifestyles they themselves aren't willing to renounce aren't just mouthing verbal noises. They realize, many of them, that the lifestyles that industrial societies provide even to their more privileged inmates are barren of meaning and value, that the pursuit and consumption of an endless series of increasingly shoddy manufactured products is a very poor substitute for a life well lived, and that stepping outside the narrowing walls of a world defined by the perks of the consumer economy is the first step toward a more meaningful existence. They know this; what they lack, by and large, is the courage to act on that knowledge, and so they wander the beach like J. Alfred Prufrock in Eliot's poem, letting the very last inch or so of the waves splash over their feet—the bottoms of their trousers rolled up carefully, to be sure, to keep them from getting wet—when they know that a running leap into the green and foaming water is the one thing that can save them. Thus it's not surprising that their daydreams cluster around imaginary tidal waves that will come rolling in from the deep ocean to sweep them away and make the whole question moot.

This is why it's as certain as anything can be that within a year or so at most, a good many of the people who spent the last decade or so talking endlessly about last Friday will have some other date lined up for the end of the world, and will talk about it just as incessantly. It's that or face up to the fact that the only way to live up to the ideals they think they espouse is to walk straight toward the thing they most fear, which is the loss of the perks and privileges and comforts that define their identity—an identity many of them hate, but still can't imagine doing without.

Meanwhile, of course, the economy, the infrastructure, and the resource flows that make those perks and privileges and comforts possible are coming apart around them. There's a great deal of wry amusement to be gained from watching one imaginary cataclysm after another seize the imagination of the peak oil scene or society as a whole, while the thing people think they're talking about—the collapse of industrial civilization—has been unfolding all around them for several years now, in exactly the way that real collapses of real civilizations happen in the real world.

Look around you, dear reader, as the economy stumbles through another round of contraction papered over with increasingly desperate fiscal gimmicks, the political system of your country moves ever deeper into dysfunction, jobs and livelihoods go away forever, whatever social safety net you're used to having comes apart, towns and neighborhoods devastated by natural disasters are abandoned rather than being rebuilt, and the basic services that once defined a modern society stop being available to a larger and larger fraction of the people of the industrial world. *This is what collapse looks like.* This is what people in the crumbling Roman Empire and all those other extinct civilizations saw when they looked out the window. To those in the middle of the process, as I've discussed in previous posts, it seems slow, but future generations with the benefit of hindsight will shake their heads in wonder at how fast industrial civilization went to pieces.

I commented in a post at the start of this year that the then-current round of fast-collapse predictions—the same predictions, mind you, that had been retailed at the start of the year before, the year before that, and so on—were not only wrong, as of course they turned out to be, but missed the collapse that was already under way. The same point holds good for the identical predictions that will no doubt be retailed over the next few weeks, insisting that this is the year when the stock market will plunge to zero, the dollar and/or the Euro will lose all their value, the economy will seize up completely and leave the grocery shelves bare, and so on endlessly; or, for that matter, that this is the year when cold fusion or algal biodiesel or some other vaporware technology will save us, or the climate change Kum Ba Ya moment I mentioned earlier will get around to happening, or what have you.

It's as safe as a bet can be that none of these things will happen in 2013, either. Here again, though, the prophecies in question are not so much wrong as irrelevant. If you're on a sinking ocean liner and the water's rising fast belowdecks, it's not exactly useful to get into heated debates with your fellow passengers about whether the ship is most likely to be vaporized by aliens or eaten by Godzilla. In the same way, it's a bit late to speculate about how industrial civilization will collapse, or how to prevent it from collapsing, when the collapse is already well under way. What matters at that stage in the game is getting some sense of how the process will unfold, not in some abstract sense but in the uncomfortably specific sense of where you are, with what you have, in the days and weeks and months and years immediately ahead of you; that, and then deciding what you are going to do about it.

With that in mind, dear reader, I'd like to ask you to do something right now, before going on to the paragraph after this one. If you're in the temperate or subarctic regions of the northern hemisphere, and you're someplace where you can adjust the temperature, get up and go turn the thermostat down three degrees; if that makes the place too chilly for your tastes, take another moment or two to put on a sweater. If you're in a different place or a different situation, do something else simple to decrease the amount of energy you're using at this moment. Go ahead, do it now; I'll wait for you here.

Have you done it? If so, you've just accomplished something that all the apocalyptic fantasies, internet debates, and protest marches of the last two decades haven't: you've decreased, by however little, the amount of carbon dioxide going into the atmosphere. That sweater, or rather the act of putting it on instead of turning up the heat, has also made you just a little less dependent on fossil fuels. In both cases, to be sure, the change you've made is very small, but a small change is better than no change at all—and a small change that can be repeated, expanded, and turned into a stepping stone on the way to bigger changes, is infinitely better than any amount of grand plans and words and handwaving that never quite manage to accomplish anything in the real world.

Turning down your thermostat, it's been said repeatedly, isn't going to save the world. That's quite true, though it's equally true that the actions that have been pursued by climate change and peak oil activists to date don't look particularly likely to save the world, either, and let's not even talk about what wasn't accomplished by all the wasted breath over last Friday's nonevent. That being the case, taking even the smallest practical steps in your own life and then proceeding from there will take you a good deal further than waiting for the mass movements that never happen, the new technologies that never pan out, or for that matter the next deus ex machina some canny marketer happens to pin onto another arbitrary date in the future, as a launching pad for the next round of apocalyptic hysteria.

Meanwhile, a world is ending. The promoters of the 2012 industry got that right, though they missed just about everything else; the process has been under way for some years now, and it won't reach its conclusion in our lifetimes, but what we may as well call the modern world is coming to an end around us. The ancient Mayans knew, however, that the end of one world is always the beginning of another, and it's an interesting detail of all the old Mesoamerican cosmological myths that the replacement for the old world doesn't just pop into being. Somebody has to take action to make the world begin.

It's a valid point, and one that can be applied to our present situation, when so many people are sitting around waiting for the end and so few seem to be willing to kickstart the beginning in the only way that matters—that is, by making actual changes in their own lives. The deindustrial world of the future is poised to begin, but someone has to begin it. Shall we?

The Next Ten Billion Years

(Originally published 4 September 2013)

Earlier this week, I was trying to think of ways to talk about the gap between notions about the future we've all absorbed from the last three hundred years of fossil-fueled progress, on the one hand, and the ways of thinking about what's ahead that might actually help us make sense of our predicament and the postpetroleum, post-progress world ahead, on the other. While I was in the middle of these reflections, a correspondent reminded me of a post from last year by peak oil blogger Ugo Bardi,[*] which set out to place the crises of our time in the context of the next ten billion years.

It's an ambitious project, and by no means badly carried out. The only criticism that comes to mind is that it only makes sense if you happen to be a true believer in the civil religion of progress, the faith whose rise and impending fall has been a central theme here in recent months. As a sermon delivered to the faithful of that religion, it's hard to beat; it's even got the classic structure of evangelical rhetoric—the awful fate that will soon fall upon those who won't change their wicked ways, the glorious salvation awaiting those who get right with Progress, and all the rest of it.

Of course the implied comparison with Christianity can only be taken so far. Christians are generally expected to humble themselves before their God, while believers in progress like to imagine that

---

[*] http://cassandralegacy.blogspot.it/2012/09/the-next-ten-billion-years.html

humanity will become God or, as in this case, be able to pat God fondly on the head and say, "That's my kid." More broadly, those of my readers who were paying attention last week will notice that the horrible fate that awaits the sinful is simply that nature will be allowed to go her own way, while the salvation awaiting the righteous is more or less the ability to browbeat nature into doing what they think she ought to do—or rather, what Bardi's hypothesized New Intelligence, whose interests are assumed to be compatible with those of humanity, thinks she ought to do.

There's plenty that could be said about the biophobia—the stark shivering dread of life's normal and healthy ripening toward death—that pervades this kind of thinking, but that's a subject for another post. Here I'd like to take another path. Once the notions of perpetual progress and imminent apocalypse are seen as industrial society's traditional folk mythologies, rather than meaningful resources for making predictions about the future, and known details about ecology, evolution, and astrophysics are used in their place to fill out the story, the next ten billion years looks very different from either of Bardi's scenarios. Here's my version or, if you will, my vision.

Ten years from now:

Business as usual continues; the human population peaks at 8.5 billion, liquid fuels production remains more or less level by the simple expedient of consuming an ever larger fraction of the world's total energy output, and the annual cost of weather-related disasters continues to rise. Politicians and the media insist loudly that better times are just around the corner, as times get steadily worse. Among those who recognize that something's wrong, one widely accepted viewpoint holds that fusion power, artificial intelligence, and interstellar migration will shortly solve all our problems, and therefore we don't have to change the way we live. Another, equally popular, insists that total human extinction is scarcely a decade away, and therefore we don't have to change the way we live. Most people accept one or the other claim, while the last chance for meaningful systemic change slips silently away.

A hundred years from now:

It has been a difficult century. After more than a dozen major wars, three bad pandemics, widespread famines, and steep worldwide declines in public health and civil order, human population is down to 3 billion and falling. Sea level is up four meters and rising fast as the Greenland and West Antarctic ice caps disintegrate; fossil fuel production ground to a halt decades earlier as the last economically producible reserves were exhausted, and most proposed alternatives turned out to be unaffordable in the absence of the sort of cheap, abundant, highly concentrated energy only fossil fuels can provide. Cornucopians still insist that fusion power, artificial intelligence, and interstellar migration will save us any day now, and their opponents still insist that human extinction is imminent, but most people are too busy trying to survive to listen to either group.

A thousand years from now:

The Earth is without ice caps and glaciers for the first time in twenty million years or so, and sea level has gone up more than a hundred meters worldwide; much of the world has a tropical climate, as it did 50 million years earlier. Human population is 100 million, up from half that figure at the bottom of the bitter dark age now passing into memory. Only a few scholars have any idea what the words "fusion power," "artificial intelligence," and "interstellar migration" once meant, and though there are still people insisting that the end of the world will arrive any day now, their arguments now generally rely more overtly on theology than before. New civilizations are rising in various corners of the world, combining legacy technologies with their own unique cultural forms. The one thing they all have in common is that the technological society of a millennium before is their idea of evil incarnate.

Ten thousand years from now:

The rise in global temperature has shut down the thermohaline circulation and launched an oceanic anoxic event, the planet's normal negative feedback process when carbon dioxide levels get out of hand. Today's industrial civilization is a dim memory from the mostly forgotten past, as far removed from this time as the Neolithic Revolution is from ours; believers in most traditional religions declare piously that the climate changes of the last ten millennia are the results of human misbehavior, while rationalists insist that this is all superstition and the climate changes have perfectly natural causes. As the anoxic oceans draw carbon out of the biosphere and entomb it in sediments on the sea floor, the climate begins a gradual cooling—a process which helps push humanity's sixth global civilization into its terminal decline.

A hundred thousand years from now:

Carbon dioxide levels drop below preindustrial levels as the oceanic anoxic event finishes its work, and the complex feedback loops that govern Earth's climate shift again: the thermohaline circulation restarts, triggering another round of climatic changes. Humanity's seventy-ninth global civilization flourishes and begins its slow decline as the disruptions set in motion by a long-forgotten industrial age are drowned out by an older climatic cycle. The scholars of that civilization are thrilled by the notions of fusion power, artificial intelligence, and interstellar migration; they have no idea that we dreamed the same dreams before them, being further in our future than the first Neanderthals are in our past, but they will have no more luck achieving those dreams than we did.

A million years from now:

The Earth is in an ice age; great ice sheets cover much of the northern hemisphere and spread from mountain ranges all over the world, and sea level is 150 meters lower than today. To the people living at this time, who have never known anything else, this seems perfectly normal. Metals have become rare geological specimens—for millennia now, most human societies have used renewable ceramic-bioplastic composites instead—and the very existence of fossil fuels has long since been forgotten. The 664th global human civilization is at its peak, lofting aerostat towns into the skies and building great floating cities on the seas; its long afternoon will eventually draw to an end after scores of generations, and when it falls, other civilizations will rise in its place.

Ten million years from now:

The long glacial epoch that began in the Pleistocene has finally ended, and the Earth is returning to its more usual status as a steamy jungle planet. This latest set of changes proves to be just that little bit too much for humanity. No fewer than 8,639 global civilizations have risen and fallen over the last ten million years, each with its own unique sciences, technologies, arts, literatures, philosophies, and ways of thinking about the cosmos; the shortest-lived lasted for less than a century before blowing itself to smithereens, while the longest-lasting endured for eight millennia before finally winding down.

All that is over now. There are still relict populations of human beings in Antarctica and a few island chains, and another million years will pass before cascading climatic and ecological changes finally push the last of them over the brink into extinction. Meanwhile, in the tropical forests of what is now southern Siberia, the descendants of raccoons who crossed the Bering land bridge during the last great ice age are proliferating rapidly, expanding into empty ecological niches once filled by the larger primates. In another thirty million years or so, their descendants will come down from the trees.

One hundred million years from now:

Retro-rockets fire and fall silent as the ungainly craft settles down on the surface of the Moon. After feverish final checks, the hatch is opened, and two figures descend onto the lunar surface. They are bipeds, but not even remotely human; instead, they belong to Earth's third intelligent species. They are distantly descended from the crows of our time, though they look no more like crows than you look like the tree shrews of the middle Cretaceous. Since you have a larynx rather than a syrinx, you can't even begin to pronounce what they call themselves, so we'll call them corvins.

Earth's second intelligent species, whom we'll call cyons after their raccoon ancestors, are long gone. They lasted a little more than eight million years before the changes of an unstable planet sent them down the long road to extinction; they never got that deeply into technology, though their political institutions made the most sophisticated human equivalents look embarrassingly crude. The corvins are another matter. Some twist of inherited psychology left them with a passion for heights and upward movement; they worked out the basic principles of the hot air balloon before they got around to inventing the wheel, and balloons, gliders, and corvin-carrying kites play much the same roles in their earliest epic literature that horses and chariots play in ours.

As corvin societies evolved more complex technologies, eyes

gazed upwards from soaring tower-cities at the Moon, the perch of perches set high above the world. All that was needed to make those dreams a reality was petroleum, and a hundred million years is more than enough time for the Earth to restock her petroleum reserves—especially if that period starts off with an oceanic anoxic event that stashes gigatons of carbon in marine sediments. Thus it was inevitable that, sooner or later, the strongest of the great corvin kith-assemblies would devote its talents and wealth to the task of reaching the Moon.

The universe has a surprise in store for the corvins, though. Their first moon landing included among its goals the investigation of some odd surface features, too small to be seen clearly by Earth-based equipment. That first lander thus set down on a flat lunar plain that, a very long time ago, was called the Sea of Tranquillity, and so it was that the stunned corvin astronauts found themselves facing the fragmentary but unmistakable remains of a spacecraft that arrived on the Moon in the unimaginably distant past.

A few equivocal traces buried in terrestrial sediments had suggested already to corvin loremasters that another intelligent species might have lived on the Earth before them, though the theory was dismissed by most as wild speculation. The shattered remnants on the Moon confirmed them, and made it hard for even the most optimistic corvins to embrace the notion that some providence guaranteed the survival of intelligent species. The curious markings on some of the remains, which some loremasters suggested might be a mode of visual communication, resisted all attempts at decipherment, and very little was ever learnt for certain about the enigmatic ancient species that left its mark on the Moon.

Even so, it will be suggested long afterwards that the stark warning embodied in those long-abandoned spacecraft played an important role in convincing corvin societies to rein in the extravagant use of petroleum and other nonrenewable resources, though it also inspired hugely expensive and ultimately futile attempts to achieve interstellar migration—for some reason the corbins never got into the quest for fusion power or artificial intelligence. One way or another, though, the corvins turned out to be the most enduring of Earth's intelligent species, and more than 28 million years passed before their day finally ended.

One billion years from now:

The Earth is old and mostly desert, and a significant fraction of its total crust is made up of the remains of bygone civilizations. The increasing heat of the Sun as it proceeds through its own life cycle, and the ongoing loss of volatile molecules from the upper atmosphere into space, have reduced the seas to scattered, salty basins amid great sandy wastes. Only near the north and south poles does vegetation flourish, and with it the corbicules, Earth's eleventh and last intelligent species. Their ancestors in our time are an invasive species of freshwater clam. (Don't laugh; a billion years ago your ancestors were still trying to work out the details of multicellularity.)

The corbicules have the same highly practical limb structure as the rest of their subphylum: six stumpy podicles for walking, two muscular dorsal tentacles for gross manipulations and two slender buccal tentacles by the mouth for fine manipulations. They spend most of their time in sprawling underground city-complexes, venturing to the surface to harvest vegetation to feed the subterranean metafungal gardens that provide them with nourishment. By some combination of luck and a broad general tendency toward cephalization common to many evolutionary lineages, Earth's last intelligent species is also its most intellectually gifted; hatchlings barely out of creche are given fun little logic problems such as Fermat's last theorem for their amusement, and a large majority of adult corbicules are involved in one or another field of intellectual endeavor. Being patient, long-lived, and not greatly addicted to collective stupidities, they have gone very far indeed.

Some eight thousand years back, a circle of radical young corbicule thinkers proposed the project of working out all the physical laws of the cosmos, starting from first principles. So unprecedented a suggestion sparked countless debates, publications, ceremonial dances, and professional duels in which elderly scholars killed themselves in order to cast unbearable opprobrium on their rivals. Still, it was far too delectable an intellectual challenge to be left unanswered, and the work has proceeded ever since. In the course of their researches, without placing any great importance on the fact, the best minds among the corbicules have proved conclusively that nuclear fusion, artificial intelligence, and interstellar migration were never practical options in the first place.

Being patient, long-lived, and not greatly addicted to collective stupidities, the corbicules have long since understood and accepted their eventual fate. In another six million years, as the Sun expands and the Earth's surface temperature rises, the last surface vegetation will perish and the corbicules will go extinct; in another ninety million years, the last multicellular life forms will die out; in another two hundred million years, the last seas will boil, and Earth's biosphere, nearing the end of its long, long life, will nestle down into the deepest crevices of its ancient, rocky world and drift into a final sleep.

Ten billion years from now:

Earth is gone. It had a splendid funeral; its body plunged into stellar fire as the Sun reached its red giant stage and expanded out to the orbit of Mars, and its ashes were flung outwards into interstellar space with the first great helium flash that marked the beginning of the Sun's descent toward its destiny. Two billion years later, the gas- and dust-rich shockwave from that flash plowed into a mass of interstellar dust dozens of light-years away from the Sun's pale corpse, and kickstarted one of the great transformative processes of the cosmos.

Billions more years have passed since that collision. A yellow-orange K-2 star now burns cheerily in the midst of six planets and two asteroid belts. The second planet has a surface temperature between the freezing and boiling points of water, and a sufficiently rich assortment of elements to set another of the great transformative processes of the cosmos into motion. Now, in one spot on the surface of this world, rising up past bulbous purplish things that don't look anything like trees but fill the same broad ecological function, there is a crag of black rock. On top of that crag, a creature sits looking at the stars, fanning its lunules with its sagittal crest and waving its pedipalps meditatively back and forth. It is one of the first members of its world's first intelligent species, and it is—for the first time ever on that world—considering the stars and wondering if other beings might live out there among them.

The creature's biochemistry, structure, and life cycle have nothing in common with yours, dear reader. Its world, its sensory organs, its mind and its feelings would be utterly alien to you, even if ten billion years didn't separate you. Nonetheless, it so happens that a few atoms that are currently part of your brain, as you read these words, will also be part of the brain-analogue of the creature on the crag on that distant, not-yet-existing world. Does that fact horrify you, intrigue you, console you, leave you cold? It's worth reflecting on that choice, and even more worth reflecting on its implications.

Man, Conqueror of Nature, Dead at 408

(Originally published 4 December 2013)

Man, the conqueror of Nature, died Monday night of a petroleum overdose, the medical examiner's office confirmed this morning. The abstract representation of the human race was 408 years old. The official announcement has done nothing to quell the rumors of suicide and substance abuse that have swirled around the death scene since the first announcement yesterday morning, adding new legal wrinkles to the struggle already under way over Man's inheritance.

Man's closest associates disagree about what happened. His longtime friend and confidant Technology thinks it was suicide. "Sure, Man liked to have a good time," he said at a press conference Tuesday evening, "and he was a pretty heavy user, but it wasn't like he was out of control or anything. No, I'm sure he did it on purpose. Just a couple of weeks ago we were hanging out at his place, looking up at the moon and talking about the trips we made out there, and he turned to me and said, 'You know, Tech, that was a good time—a really good time. I wonder if I'll ever do anything like that again.' He got into moods like that more and more often in the last few years. I tried to cheer him up, talking about going to Mars or what have you, and he'd go along with it but you could tell his heart wasn't in it."

Other witnesses told a different story. "It was terrifying," said a housekeeper who requested that her name not be given. "He was using more and more of the stuff every day, shooting it up morning, noon and night, and when his connections couldn't get him as much as he wanted, he'd go nuts. You'd hear him screaming at the top of his lungs and pounding his fists on the walls. Everybody on the staff would hide whenever that happened, and it happened more and more often—the amount he was using was just unbelievable. Some of his friends tried to talk him into getting help, or even just cutting back a little on his petroleum habit, but he wouldn't listen."

The medical examiner's office and the police are investigating Man's death right now. Until their report comes out, the tragic end of humanity's late self-image remains shrouded in mystery and speculation.

A Tumultuous Family Saga

"He was always a rebel," said Clio, the muse of history, in an exclusive interview in her office on Mount Helicon this morning. "That was partly his early environment, of course. He was born in the household of Sir Francis Bacon, remember, and brought up by some of the best minds of seventeenth-century Europe; an abstract image of humanity raised by people like that wasn't likely to sit back and leave things as they were. Still, I think there were strong family influences too. His father was quite the original figure himself, back in the day."

Though almost forgotten nowadays, Man's father Everyman, the abstract representation of medieval humanity, was as mediagenic in his own time as his son became later on. The star of a wildly popular morality play and the subject of countless biographies, Everyman was born in extreme poverty in a hovel in post-Roman Europe, worked his way up to become a wealthy and influential figure in the Middle Ages and Renaissance, then stepped aside from his financial and political affairs to devote his last years to religious concerns.

Savage quarrels between father and son kept the broadsheet and pamphlet press fed with juicy stories all through the seventeenth and eighteenth centuries, and eventually led to their final breach over Darwin's theory of evolution in 1859.

By that time Man was already having problems with substance abuse. "He was just using coal at first," Technology reminisced. "Well, let's be fair, we both were. That was the hot new drug in those days. It was cheap, you could get it without too much hassle, and everybody on the cutting edge was using it. I remember one trip we took together—it was on one of the early railroads, at thirty miles an hour. We thought that was really fast. Were we innocent back then, or what?"

Clio agreed with that assessment. "I don't think Man had any idea what he was getting into, when he started abusing coal," she said. "It was an easy habit to fall into, very popular in avant-garde circles just then, and nobody yet knew much about the long term consequences of fossil fuel abuse. Then, of course, he started his campaign to conquer Nature, and he found out very quickly that he couldn't keep up the pace he'd set for himself without artificial help. That was when the real tragedy began."

The Conquest of Nature

It's an open question when Man first decided to conquer Nature. "The biographers all have their own opinions on that," Clio explained, gesturing at a shelf loaded with books on Man's dramatic and controversial career. "Some trace it back to the influence of his foster-father Francis Bacon, or the other mentors and teachers he had in his early days. Others say that the inspiration came from the crowd he ran with when he was coming of age in the eighteenth and nineteenth centuries. He used to tell interviewers that it was a family thing, that everyone in his family all the way back to the Stone Age had been trying to conquer Nature and he was just the one who finally succeeded, but that won't stand up to any kind of scrutiny. Examine the career of Everyman, for example, and you'll find that he wasn't interested in conquering Nature; he wanted to conquer himself."

"The business about conquering Nature?" Technology said. "He got into that back when we were running around being young and crazy. I think he got the idea originally from his foster-father or one of the other old guys who taught him when he was a kid, but as far as I know it wasn't a big deal to him until later. Now I could be wrong, you know. I didn't know him that well in those days; I was mostly just doing my thing then, digging mines, building water mills, stuff like that. We didn't get really close until we both got involved in this complicated coal deal; we were both using, but I was dealing, too, and I could get it cheaper than anybody else—I was using steam, and none of the other dealers knew how to do that. So we got to be friends and we had some really wild times together, and now and then when we were good and ripped, he'd get to talking about how Nature ought to belong to him and one of these days he was going to hire some soldiers and just take it.

"Me, I couldn't have cared less, except that Man kept on bringing me these great technical problems, really sweet little puzzles, and I've always been a sucker for those. He figured out how I was getting the coal for him so cheap, you see, and guessed that I could take those same tricks and use them for his war against Nature. For me, it was just a game, for Nature, against Nature, I couldn't care less. Just give me a problem and let me get to work on it, and I'm happy.

"But it wasn't just a game for him. I think it was 1774 when he really put me to work on it. He'd hired some mercenaries by then, and was raising money and getting all kind of stuff ready for the war. He wanted steam engines so, like the man said, it was steam engine time—I got working on factories, railroads, steamships, all the rest. He already had some of his people crossing the border into Nature to seize bits of territory before then, but the eighteenth century, that's when the invasion started for real. I used to stand next to him at the big rallies he liked to hold in those days, with all the soldiers standing in long lines, and he'd go into these wild rants about the glorious future we were going to see once Nature was conquered. The soldiers loved it; they'd cheer and grab their scientific instruments and lab coats and go conquer another province of Nature."

The Triumphant Years

It was in 1859, Technology recalled, that Man first started using petroleum. "He'd just had the big spat with his dad over this Darwin dude: the worst fight they ever had, and in fact Man never spoke to the old guy again. Man was still steaming about the fight for days afterwards, and then we heard that this guy named Edwin Drake over in Pennsylvania could get you something that was an even bigger rush than coal. Of course Man had to have some, and I said to myself, hey, I'll give it a try—and that was all she wrote, baby. Oh, we kept using coal, and a fair bit of it, but there's nothing like petroleum.

"What's more, Man figured out that that's what he needed to finish his conquest of Nature. His mercs had a good chunk of Nature by then, but not all of it, not even half, and Man was having trouble holding some of the territory he'd taken—there were guerrillas behind his lines, that sort of thing. He'd pace around at headquarters, snapping at his staff, trying to figure out how to get the edge he needed to beat Nature once and for all. 'I've gotta have it all, Tech,' he'd say sometimes, when we were chilling on the couch in his private quarters, with a couple of needles and a barrel of petroleum, getting really buzzed. 'I've conquered distance, the land, the surface of the sea—it's not enough. I want it *all*.' And you know, he got pretty close."

Petroleum was the key, Clio explained. "It wasn't just that Man used petroleum, all his soldiers and his support staff were using it too, and over the short term it's an incredibly powerful drug; it gives users a rush of energy that has to be seen to be believed. Whole provinces of Nature that resisted every attack in the first part of the war were overrun once Man started shipping petroleum to his forces. By the 1950s, as a result, the conquest of Nature was all but complete. Nature still had a few divisions holed up in isolated corners where they couldn't be gotten at by Man's forces, and partisan units were all over the conquered zone, but those were minor irritations at that point. It was easy enough for Man and his followers to convince themselves that in a little while the last holdouts would be defeated and Nature would be conquered once and for all.

"That's when reality intervened, though, because all those years of abusing coal, petroleum, and other substances started to catch up with Man. He was in bad shape, and didn't know it—and then he started having problems feeding his addiction."

On and Off the Wagon

"I forget exactly how it happened," Technology recounted. "It was some kind of disagreement with his suppliers—he was getting a lot of his stuff from some Arab guys at that point, and he got into a fight with them over something, and they said, 'Screw you, man, if you're going to be like that we're just not going to do business with you any more.' So he tried to get the stuff from somebody else, and it turned out the guy from Pennsylvania was out of the business, and the connections he had in Texas and California couldn't get enough. The Arab guys had a pretty fair corner on the market. So Man went into withdrawal, big time. We got him to the hospital, and the doctor took one look at him and said, 'You gotta get into rehab, now.' So me and some of his other friends talked him into it."

"The records of his stays in rehab are heartbreaking," Clio said, pulling down a tell-all biography from her shelf. "He'd start getting the drug out of his system, convince himself that he was fine, check himself out, and start using again almost immediately. Then, after a little while, he'd have problems getting a fix, end up in withdrawal, and find his way back into rehab. Meanwhile the war against Nature was going badly as the other side learned how to fight back effectively. There were rumors of ceasefire negotiations, even a peace treaty between him and Nature."

"I went to see him in rehab one day," said Technology. "He looked awful. He looked *old*—like his dad Everyman. He was depressed, too, talking all the time about this malaise thing. The thing is, I think if he'd stuck with it then he could have gotten off the stuff and straightened his life out. I really think he could have done it, and I tried to help. I brought him some solar panels, earth-sheltered housing, neat stuff like that, to try to get him interested in something besides the war on Nature and his petroleum habit. That seemed to cheer him up, and I think all his friends had high hopes for a while.

"Then the next thing I heard, he was out of rehab. He just couldn't hack it any longer. I went to his place, and there he was, laughing and slapping everybody's back and full of big ideas and bigger plans, just like before. That's what it looked like at first, but the magic was gone. He tried to do a comeback career, but he just couldn't get it back together, and things went downhill from there."

The Final Years

The last years of Man's career as representation of the human race were troubled. "The war against Nature wasn't going well by then," Clio explained. "Man's forces were holding onto the most important provinces and cities, but insurgencies were springing up all over—drug-resistant microbes here, herbicide-tolerant weeds there. Morale was faltering, and a growing fraction of Man's forces in the struggle against Nature no longer believed in what they were doing. They were in it for the money, nothing more, and the money was running out. Between the costs of the war, the costs of Man's lavish lifestyle, and the rising burden of his substance abuse problem, Man was in deep financial trouble; there's reason to believe that he may have been engaged in outright fraud to pay his bills during the last few years of his life."

Meanwhile, Man was becoming increasingly isolated. "He'd turned his back on most of his friends," said the anonymous housekeeper quoted earlier. "Art, Literature, Philosophy—he stopped talking to any of them, because they kept telling him to get off the stuff and straighten out his life. I remember the last time Science came to visit—she wanted to talk to Man about what he was doing to the atmosphere, and Man literally threw her out of the house and slammed the door in her face. I was working downstairs in the laundry, where you usually can't hear much, but I could hear Man screaming, 'I own the atmosphere! I own the planet! I own the solar system! I own the goddamn *stars*! They're mine, mine, *mine*— how dare you tell me what to do with my property?' He went on like that for a while, then collapsed right there in the entry. A couple of us went up, carried him into his bedroom, and got him cleaned up and put to bed. We had to do that pretty often, the last year or so."

His longtime friend Technology was apparently the last person to see Man alive. "I went over to his place Monday afternoon," Technology recalled. "I went there pretty often, and we'd do some stuff and hang out, and I'd start rapping about all kinds of crazy stuff, omniscient supercomputers, immortal robot bodies, stuff like that. I told him, 'Look, Man, if you want to get into stuff like omniscience and immortality, go talk to Religion. That's her bag, not mine.' But he didn't want to do that; he had some kind of falling out with her a while back, you know, and he wanted to hear it from me, so I talked it up. It got him to mellow out and unwind, and that's what mattered to me.

"Monday, though, we get to talking, and it turns out that the petroleum he had was from this really dirty underground source in North Dakota. I said to him, 'Man, what the frack were you thinking?' He just looked at me and said, 'I've gotta have the stuff, Tech. I've gotta have the stuff.' Then he started blubbering, and I reached out to, like, pat his shoulder—and he just blew up at me. He started yelling about how it was my fault he was hooked on petroleum, my fault the war against Nature wasn't going well, my fault this and that and blah blah blah. Then he got up and stormed out of the room and slammed the door behind him. I should have gone after him, I know I should have, but instead I just shook my head and left. Maybe if I'd gone and tried to talk him down, he wouldn't have done it."

"Everything was quiet," the housekeeper said. "Too quiet. Usually we'd hear Man walking around, or he'd put some music on or something, but Monday night, the place might as well have been empty. Around ten o' clock, we were really starting to wonder if something was wrong, and two of us from the housekeeping staff decided that we really had to go check on Man and make sure he was all right. We found him in the bathroom, lying on the floor. It was horrible—the room stank of crude oil, and there was the needle and all his other gear scattered around him on the floor. We tried to find a pulse, but he was already cold and stiff; I went and called for an ambulance anyway, and—well, you know the rest."

The Troubled Aftermath

Man's death leaves a great many questions unanswered. "By the time Everyman died," Clio explained, "everyone knew who his heir would be. Man had already taken over his father's role as humanity's idealized self-image. That hasn't happened this time, as you know. Man didn't leave a will, and his estate is a mess—it may be years before the lawyers and the accountants finish going through his affairs and figure out whether there's going to be anything at all for potential heirs to claim. Meanwhile there are at least half a dozen contenders for the role of abstract representation of the human race, and none of them is a clear favorite. It may be a long time before all the consequences are sorted out."

Meanwhile, one of the most important voices in the debate has already registered an opinion. Following her invariable habit, Gaia refused to grant any personal interviews, but a written statement to the media was delivered by a spokesrabbit on Tuesday evening. "Please accept My sympathy for the tragic demise of Man, the would-be conqueror of Nature," it read. "I hope it will not be out of place, though, to suggest that whomever My human children select as their new self-image might consider being a little less self-centered—not to mention a little less self-destructive."

A Christmas Speculation

(Originally published 25 December 2013)

Regular readers of this blog will be aware that I've spent most of the last year discussing the place of religion in the troubled future ahead of us.[*] This holiday season, in which millions of Americans have just engaged in an all-out orgy of conspicuous consumption and mindless waste to celebrate the birth of a poor carpenter's son in a stable in Bethlehem, also has me thinking about religious matters, and it occurs to me that there's an issue along these lines that my blog posts haven't yet explored. It may not have much to do with the future of the modern industrial world, but it may just explain a thing or two about the present and the recent past here in the United States.

I'm sorry to say that the issue I have in mind has a distinct partisan dimension, which marks a break from my usual policy in this blog. One of the more common criticisms I field from irate readers, in fact, is the insistence that I treat politicians of both major US parties as though they're interchangeable. It's a valid criticism, since I do indeed do this, and the only justification I can offer is that, by and large, that's the way they behave. For exhibit A, it's hard to beat the current inmate of the White House, who won the presidency just over five years ago in a flurry of sound bites about "hope" and "change," and then turned around and gave us a truly inspired

---

[*]   The series of posts mentioned here became the raw material for my book *After Progress*.

imitation of the third and fourth terms of George W. Bush, complete with all the drone strikes and violations of civil liberties that his chorus of sycophants in the media used to insist he was sure to abolish once he got into office.

Still, the criticism has some merit, since there's one significant difference between the two major US parties. Most Democratic politicians, like the example just cited, will say and do whatever it takes to get elected, and then conveniently forget all about their alleged ideals in order to proceed with, and profit from, the ordinary business of politics once they land in office. A fair number of Republican politicians do exactly the same thing, to be sure, but there's also a large number of Republicans who have convictions regarding important social issues, and cling firmly to those convictions even when they're not popular. That's a distinction worth noting, but a certain amount of confusion enters the picture when the Republicans in question—as nearly all of them do—insist that their convictions follow from their Christian faith.

Now of course the Christian faith does have quite a bit to say about social issues. Theologies differ from church to church, but friends of mine in several different denominations assure me that the words of Jesus quoted in the four gospels of the New Testament are considered definitive guides to faith and morals, so I sat down a few days ago with a copy of the King James version and spent an afternoon reading the gospels—not, by the way, for the first time. Here are the passages I found in which Jesus tells his followers that they have a duty to take care of children, the poor, and other vulnerable people:

Matthew 18:6, 18:10, 19:21, 23:14, and 25:31-46; Mark 9:36-37, 10:21, and 12:40; and Luke 10:30-37, 11:41, 12:33, 14:12-14, 18:22, and 20:47.

Here are the passages in which Jesus tells his followers to pay their taxes without complaining:

Matthew 5:42, 17:24-27, and 22:19-21; Mark 12:14-17; and Luke 6:30 and 20:21-25.

Here are the passages in which Jesus tells his followers that they aren't supposed to obsess about other people's sins, but should leave that to God, and attend to their own moral failings instead:

Matthew 7:1-5 and 9:10-13; Mark 2:15-17; Luke 6:37, 6:41-42, 7:44-48, 15:2, 18:10-14, and 19:7; and John 8:2-11.

And here are the passages in which Jesus tells his followers to blame the poor and vulnerable for their plight, direct benefits toward the already well-to-do at the expense of everyone else, refuse to pay their fair share of taxes, and obsessively denounce and punish the sins of people they don't like while finding every opportunity to excuse their own sins and those of their friends:

Yet these latter are the things that a great many Republicans, and in particular a great many of those Republicans who claim to be motivated by their Christian faith, have been pursuing in practice, if not always advocating in theory. If they're deriving their commitments from a religion, it's pretty clearly not the one taught by Jesus. Many people have made this same point in recent years, but it doesn't seem to have occurred to any of them that another religion that's active in today's America does teach all the things the GOP supports. That religion, of course, is Satanism, and more specifically the version of it taught in Anton Szandor LaVey's *The Satanic Bible*.

Those who were around during LaVey's glory days in the 1970s, when he appeared regularly on talk shows and had a coterie of Hollywood stars in his Church of Satan, will doubtless remember *The Satanic Bible*. For those who weren't, it's a book-length screed denouncing Christian morality and upholding an ethic of raw selfishness and might-makes-right. It's still very much in copyright, so I'm not going to quote it here, but any reader who turns its pages will find the present social policy of the GOP precisely reflected in LaVey's dismissal of two thousand years of Christian teaching about our duty to care for one another, his shrill denunciations of the vulnerable and needy as "parasites" and "vampires," and his insistence that the successful owe nothing to anybody else.

An interesting coincidence, or perhaps an ironic one? Maybe so, but I find myself wondering if there's more to it than that. It happens fairly often that the repeated failure of a belief system causes many former believers to swing all the way to the opposite extreme, and embrace the antithesis of their former faith. The neoconservatives who briefly and disastrously shaped the direction of US foreign policy in the first years of this century are a case in point: many of the leaders of that movement were doctrinaire Marxists during their college years, and responded to the abject failure of Marxism by doing their level best to become the wicked capitalists they had once so fervently denounced.

The evangelical revival of the late 1970s and 1980s, in turn, was pervaded by hopes at least as extreme and unrealistic as anything the Marxists envisioned in their heyday. Wildly popular books such as Hal Lindsey's *The Late Great Planet Earth* convinced millions of newly "Born Again" Christians that the Second Coming was due any minute, and the repeated failure of Jesus to show up on cue must have put immense psychological strains on a great many people who cut their ties to the secular world in the imminent expectation of Armageddon. All through those same years, in turn, copies of *The Satanic Bible* could be found in cheap mass market editions on the shelves of chain bookstores all over America. It's not hard to imagine how, after each loudly proclaimed date for the Rapture waltzed serenely by without incident, a trickle of not-quite-former fundamentalists could well have responded to their feelings of humiliation and despair by walking away from the Bible section in those same bookstores and seeing if the opposing side had something better on offer.

Those who found solace of one sort or another in LaVey's evocation of diabolical values would have had several good reasons not to make their change of heart public, to be sure. On the one hand (or horn, or cloven hoof), a public confession of devil worship would have been difficult to explain to one's employer in those somewhat more innocent times, and the reactions of one's presumably Christian friends and family would also have been an issue for many. On the other, one of the classic titles given Satan by Christian theologians is "the father of lies," and it's easy to see how the thought of remaining ostensibly Christian while practicing devil worship in private, and perhaps leading others down the Left Hand Path, might have seemed like the most delectable option available to these new Satanic converts.

Nor would active membership in most of today's Christian churches have been any impediment to the enthusiastic worship of Satan. According to Matthew 7:21, it's not enough to say "Lord, Lord," to qualify as a Christian; it's also necessary to do the will of God—a requirement that, as noted above, involves among other things some highly specific commitments to help the poor and vulnerable. Thus covert devil worshippers could shout "Jesus is Lord" at the top of their lungs every Sunday, and so long as they carefully refrained from following the teachings of the gospels, they would have had no difficulty maintaining their status as Satanists in good standing. This, it seems, they accordingly did.

As the number of devil worshippers in evangelical churches and the Christian end of the Republican Party increased, though, their most pressing need would have been some surreptitious way to signal their involvement to those who shared their convictions, without believers in the Christian gospel being any the wiser. Coming up with a Satanic shibboleth that would be instantly recognizable to other devil worshippers, but completely opaque to devout Christians, might seem like a tall order, but it's one that seems to have been met with aplomb.

Yes, this is where we discuss Ayn Rand.

All things considered, Rand's cult status in those circles that call themselves conservative these days is hard to explain, because Rand was not a conservative. By that I don't simply mean that she rejected the term and savagely denounced conservative ideas and politicians, though this is true; nor that the conservative movement in her time rejected her ideas with at least as much energy as she did theirs, and generally with better logic than hers, though this was also the case. Far more important here is that she was a radical ideologue of exactly the sort against which the founders of conservatism directed their most barbed and thoughtful critiques.

As discussed in Russell Kirk's brilliant study *The Conservative Mind*, classical conservatism has at its core an enduring and wholly justified suspicion of claims that some abstract ideology or other can bring about heaven on earth. "The pretended rights of these theorists," wrote Edmund Burke, "are all extremes; and in proportion as they are metaphysically true, they are morally and politically false." He was talking about the Jacobins, but he could just as well have been talking about Rand.

Still, there's another point that is worth making here, which is that Ayn Rand was a violent opponent of Christianity and Christian morality, a committed atheist who considered selfishness a central moral virtue, and who also idolized one of the most disgusting child murderersof the twentieth century.[*] Her present role as intellectual pin-up girl for people who call themselves Christian conservatives is

---

[*] See, for example, http://michaelprescott.freeservers.com/romancing-the-stone-cold.html

thus a little odd, since claiming to be a Christian and a believer in Rand's teachings at the same time is right up there with claiming to be a vegetarian carnivore or a celibate harlot. It's not just that one of these things is not like the other; Rand's teachings are flatly, openly, and deliberately opposed to every part of the gospel of Jesus.

Rand's anticommunism made her turgid novels popular on the less thoughtful end of the American right in the 1950s and 1960s, though, and that accident of history prepared her for what might just be her core role in contemporary culture: a covert way for devil worshippers to identify themselves to one another in the supposedly Christian (and just as supposedly conservative) GOP of today. Closet Satanists attending fundamentalist church services or Republican party get-togethers can't exactly sport upside-down pentagrams on their shirts or greet other attendees with a hearty "Hail Satan," but a casual reference to one of Rand's novels or pseudophilosophical screeds is the next best thing: once someone else responds enthusiastically to the mention of Rand's name, a few other seemingly casual comments and perhaps a covert devil sign or two would be enough to settle the matter.

All this may suggest some sobering reflections as we approach the beginning of another US election year, in which most races will pit a candidate from a party that puts its faith in Lucifer against a candidate from a party that for all practical purposes believes in nothing at all. Still, when supposedly Christian politicians start waxing rhapsodic about the alleged intellectual or literary virtues of Ayn Rand, I trust my readers will remember that what they're saying actually works out to "I worship the Prince of Darkness, and you should too!" Any of my readers who happen to be devil worshippers themselves can proceed to welcome them as friends and brothers, while those of other faiths can cast their votes as their own ethical views suggest.

On the off chance that any Republican Satanists are reading these lines, though, I'd like to offer a helpful suggestion. The long charade of pretending to be Christian conservatives has no doubt been great fun, and it's certainly succeeded in getting Satanic ideas widely accepted all through those parts of American society that might have been expected to resist them most forcefully. Only one of the seven deadly sins has gotten by without extravagant praise from so-called Christian conservatives in recent years—it's hard to glorify an economic system that depends on avarice, gluttony, envy and sloth, and a foreign policy defined by pride and wrath, in any other way— and no doubt they'll find a way to fit lust in there somewhere one of these days, and finish collecting the whole set.

At this point, though, it's hard to see any reason why the Satanists in the GOP need to keep the pretense going any longer. In an era when most discussions of the Christmas season in the mass media fixate on whether retailers are making a big enough profit to keep the economy stumbling blindly onward for one more year, I think a strong case can be made that America is ready to shake off the last of its qualms and openly embrace a Satanic political agenda. Among its other benefits, putting public devil worship at the heart of the GOP, where it so evidently belongs, can't help but improve the flagging ratings of Republican national conventions; the otherwise tedious proceedings of the 2016 GOP convention, for example, would be enlivened no end by a Black Mass celebrated by the GOP nominee, perhaps with Ann Coulter's nude form draped over the altar and a chorus of delegates chanting "Evil, be thou my good!" from the bleachers.

In the meantime, I would like to wish to those of my readers who actually believe in the gospel of Jesus, who study his teachings prayerfully and try their level best to live their lives in accordance with them, a very merry Christmas; to my other readers, blessings on whatever holiday you celebrate in this season of hope's rebirth in a cold and bitter time; and to all, a happy new year.

The Crocodiles of Reality

(Originally published 12 March 2014)

I've suggested in several previous posts that the peak oil debate may be approaching a turning point—one of those shifts in the collective conversation in which topics that have been shut out for years or decades finally succeed in crashing the party, and other topics that have gotten more than their quota of attention during that time get put out to pasture or sent to the glue factory. I'd like to talk for a moment about some of the reasons I think that's about to happen, and in the process, give a name to one of the common but generally unmentionable features of contemporary economic life.

We can begin with the fracking bubble, that misbegotten brat fathered by Wall Street's love of Ponzi schemes on Main Street's stark terror of facing up to the end of the age of cheap abundant energy. That bubble has at least two significant functions in today's world. The first function, as discussed in these essays already, is to fill an otherwise vacant niche in the string of giddy speculative delusions that began with the stock market boom and bust of 1987 and is still going strong today. As with previous examples, the promoters of the fracking bubble dangled the prospect of what used to be normal returns on investment in front of the eager and clueless investors with which America seems to be so richly stocked these days. These then leapt at the bait, and handed their money over to the tender mercies of the same Wall Street investment firms who gave us Pets.com and zero-doc mortgages.

You might think, dear reader, that after a quarter century of this, there might be a shortage of chumps willing to fall for such schemes. Whatever else might be depleting, though, the supply of lambs eager to be led to that particular slaughter seems to be keeping up handily with the demand. We live in what will doubtless be remembered as the Golden Age of financial fraud, an era of stunning fiscal idiocy in which even the most blatant swindles can count on drawing a crowd of suckers begging to have their money taken from them. Millennia from now, the grifters, con men, and bunco artists of civilizations yet unborn will look back in awe at our time, and wish that they, too, might be fortunate enough to live in an era when tens of millions of investors passionately wanted to believe that the laws of economics, thermodynamics, and plain common sense must surely be suspended for their benefit.

To some extent, in other words, the fracking bubble is simply one more reminder that Ben Franklin's adage about a fool and his money has not lost any of its relevance since the old rascal slipped it into the pages of *Poor Richard's Almanac*. Still, there's more going on here than the ruthless fleecing of the unwary that's the lifeblood of every healthy market economy. The fracking bubble, as most of my readers will be well aware, has not only served as an excuse for ordinary speculative larceny; it's also provided a very large number of people with an excuse to scrunch up their eyes, stuff their fingers in their ears, shout "La, la, la, I can't hear you," and thus keep clinging to the absurd faith that limitless resources really can be extracted from a finite planet.

For the last three or four years, accordingly, the fracking bubble has been the most common item brandished by practitioners of peak oil denial as evidence that petroleum production can *too* keep on increasing forever, so there! The very modest additions to global petroleum production that resulted from hydrofracturing shales in North Dakota and Texas got talked up into an imaginary tidal wave of crude oil that would supposedly sweep all before it, and not incidentally restore the United States to its long-vanished status as the world's premier oil producer. All that made good copy for the bunco artists mentioned earlier, to be sure, but it also fed into the futile attempts at denial that have taken the place of a sane energy policy in most industrial societies.

The problem with this fond fantasy is that the numbers don't even begin to add up. Each year, on average, the oil industry has had had to increase its investments by 10% over the previous year to get the same amount of oil out of the ground. Even $100-a-barrel oil prices won't support that kind of soaring overhead cost for long, and the problem has been made worse by the belated discovery that many of the shale beds ballyhooed in recent years don't have anything like as much oil as their promoters claimed. As a result, oil companies around the world are cutting back on capital investment and selling off assets. That's not the behavior of an industry poised on the brink of a new age of abundance; it's the behavior of an industry that has just slammed face first into hard supply limits and is backing away groggily from the impact site while trying to stanch the bleeding from deep fiscal cuts.

As a result, with mathematical certainty, a great many overpriced assets are going to lose most of their paper value in the years ahead of us, a great many businesses that have made their money providing goods and services to the drilling industry are going to downsize sharply or simply go bankrupt, a great many wells that can't make money even at exorbitant oil prices are going to be shut in or go undrilled in the first place, and a very, very great number of people who convinced themselves that they were going to get rich by investing in fracking are going to end up poor. It's not going to be pretty. Exactly what effect this is going to have on the price of oil is an interesting question; my guess, though it's only a guess, is that a couple of years from now the price of oil will spike, possibly to the $250-$300 a barrel range, then crash to $60 a barrel, and slowly recover to $175 or so over a period of several years.

This has a great deal of relevance to the project of this blog. The last time petroleum production failed to keep pace with potential demand, and the price of oil spiked accordingly, peak oil came in from the fringes and got discussed publicly in the pages of newspapers of record. That window of opportunity gaped open from 2004 to 2010, roughly speaking, and during that period a great deal got accomplished. That was when peak oil stopped being a concern of the furthest fringe and found an audience in many corners of contemporary alternative culture, when local groups—some under the Transition Town banner, others outside it—began to organize around the imminence of peak oil, and when books on resource depletion and its consequences found a market for the first time since the early 1980s.

Those are significant gains. It's true, of course, that these achievements didn't make peak oil go away, or find some gimmick that will keep the lifestyles of the industrial world's more privileged inmates rolling merrily along for the foreseeable future. What sometimes gets forgotten is that neither of those things was ever possible in the first place. The hard facts of our predicament have not changed a bit: the age of cheap abundant energy is ending; the economic systems, social structures, and lifestyle habits that were made possible by that temporary condition are accordingly going away, and nothing anyone can do will bring them back again, not now, not ever.

It's worth being precise here: for the rest of the time our species endures, we will have to deal with much more sharply constrained energy supplies than we've had handy over the last few centuries. That doesn't mean that our descendants will be condemned to huddle in caves until the jaws of extinction close around them; I've argued at quite some length in one of my books[*] that the endpoint of the mess we're currently in, centuries from now, will most likely be the emergence of ecotechnic societies—societies that maintain relatively

---

[*] *The Ecotechnic Future.*

high technology on the modest energy and resource inputs that can be provided by renewable sources. I've suggested, there and elsewhere, that there's quite a bit that can be done here and now to lay the foundations for the ecotechnic societies of the far future. I've also tried to point out that there's quite a bit that can be done here and now to make the unraveling of the age of abundance less traumatic than it will otherwise be.

To my mind, those are worthwhile goals. What makes them difficult is simply that any meaningful attempt to pursue them has to start by accepting that the age of cheap abundant energy is ending, that the lifestyles that age made possible are ending with it, and that wasting all those fossil fuels on what amounts to a drunken binge three centuries long might not have been a very smart idea in the first place. Any one of those would be a bitter pill to take; all three of them together are far more than most people nowadays are willing to swallow, and so it's not surprising that so much effort over the last few decades have gone into pretending that the squalid excesses of contemporary culture can somehow keep rolling along in the teeth of all the evidence to the contrary.

The frantic attempts to sustain the unsustainable driven by this pretense have done much to make the present day such a halcyon time for swindles of every description. Not all of those, however, have taken aim at the wallets of what we might as well call the lumpen-investmentariat, that class of people who have money to invest and not a clue in their heads that Wall Street might not have their best interests at heart. Some of the most colorful flops of recent years have instead attracted money from a different though equally gullible source: government subsidies for new energy technologies.

Those of my readers who were part of the peak oil scene a decade ago, for example, may remember the days when ethanol made from American corn was going to save us all. Many of the same claims more recently deployed to inflate the fracking bubble were used to justify what was described, at the time, as America's burgeoning new ethanol industry, but the target for these exercises was somewhat different. A certain amount of investment money from the clueless did find its way into the hands of ethanol-plant promoters, to be sure, but the financial core of the new industry was a flurry of federal mandates and federal and state subsidies, which in theory existed to lead America to a bright new energy future, and in practice existed to convince the voters that politicians really were doing something about gasoline prices that had just risen to the unheard-of level of $2 a gallon.

You won't hear much about America's burgeoning new ethanol industry these days. A substantial fraction of the ethanol plants that were subsidized by governments and lavishly praised by politicians a decade ago are bankrupt and shuttered today, having failed to turn a profit or, in some cases, cover the costs of construction. The critics who pointed out that the burgeoning new industry made no economic sense, and that making ethanol from corn uses more energy than you get from burning the ethanol, turned out to be dead right, and the critics who dismissed them as naysayers turned out to be dead wrong. Still, the ethanol plants accomplished the same two functions as the fracking bubble did later: they sucked a great deal of money into the hands of their promoters, and helped everyone else pretend for a while that the end of the age of cheap abundant energy wasn't going to happen after all.

It's hardly the only example of the phenomenon. Since I don't want green-energy proponents to feel unduly picked on, let's turn to the other side of the energy picture and take a look at nuclear fusion. Since the 1950s, a sizeable body of nuclear physicists have kept themselves gainfully employed and their laboratories stocked and staffed by proclaiming nuclear fusion as the wave of the future. In just another twenty years, we've repeatedly been told, clean, safe nuclear fusion plants will be churning out endless supplies of energy, if only the government subsidies keep pouring in. After sixty years of unbroken failure, even politicians are starting to have second thoughts, but the fusion-power industry keeps at it, pursuing a project that, as respected science writer Charles Seife pointed out trenchantly in his book *Sun In A Bottle: The Strange History of Fusion and the Science of Wishful Thinking*, has more in common with the quest for perpetual motion than its overeager fans like to think.

Every few years the media thus carries yet another enthusiastic announcement that some new breakthrough has happened in the quest for fusion power. Now of course it's worth noting that none of these widely ballyhooed breakthroughs ever amount to a working fusion reactor capable of putting power into the grid, but let's let that pass for now, because the point I want to make is a different one. As I pointed out in a post here last year, the question that matters about fusion is not whether fusion power is technically feasible, but whether it's economically viable. That's not a question anyone in the fusion research industry wants to discuss, and there are good reasons for that.

The ITER project in Europe offers a glimpse at the answer. ITER is the most complex and also the most expensive machine ever built by human beings—the latest estimate of the total cost has recently gone up from $14 billion to $17 billion, and if past performance is anything to go by, it will have gone up a good deal more before the scheduled completion in 2020. That stratospheric price tag results from the simple fact that six decades of hard work by physicists around the world, exploring scores of different approaches to fusion, have shown that any less expensive approach won't produce a sustained fusion reaction. While commercial fusion reactors would doubtless cost less than ITER, it's already clear that they won't cost enough less to make fusion power economically viable. Even if ITER succeeds in creating its "sun in a bottle," in other words, that fact will be an expensive laboratory curiosity, not a solution to the world's energy needs.

My more attentive readers will doubtless have noticed that the flaw in the current round of glowing prophecies of a future powered by fusion plants is the same as the flaw in the equally glowing sales pitches for corn-based ethanol fuel plants a decade ago. Turning corn into ethanol, and using the ethanol to fuel cars and trucks, is technically feasible; it just doesn't happen to be economically viable. In the same way, whether fusion power is technically feasible or not may still be up in the air, but the question of its economic viability is not. The gap between technical capacity and economic reality provides the ecological niche in which both these projects make their home, and a great many other alleged solutions to the energy crisis of our time exploit that same niche.

I'd like to suggest that it's high time to put a name to the technological fauna that fill this role in our social ecology, and I even have a name to propose. I think we should call them "subsidy dumpsters."

A subsidy dumpster, if I may venture on a definition, is an energy technology that looks like a viable option so long as nobody pays attention to the economic realities. Because it's technically feasible, or at least hasn't yet been proven to be unfeasible, promoters can brandish enthusiastic estimates of how much energy it will yield if only the government provides adequate funding, and point to laboratory tests of technical feasibility as evidence that so tempting a bait is within reach. The promoters of such schemes can also rely on the foam-flecked ravings of economists, who have proven to be so stunningly clueless about energy in recent years, and they can also count on one of the pervasive blind spots in modern thinking: the almost visceral inability of most people these days to think in terms of whole systems. Armed with these advantages, they descend upon politicians, and if energy costs are an irritation to the public—and these days, energy costs are *always* an irritation to the public—the politicians duly cough up a subsidy so they can claim to be doing something about the energy problem.

Once the subsidy dumpster gets its funding, it goes through

however many twists and turns its promoters can manage before economic realities take their inevitable toll. If the dumpster in question has to compete in the marketplace, as fuel ethanol plants did, the normal result is a series of messy bankruptcies as soon as the government money runs short. If it can be shielded from the market, preferably by always being almost ready for commercial deployment but never actually quite getting there—the fusion-research industry has this one down pat, though it's fair to say that the laws of nature seem to be giving them a great deal of help—the dumpster can keep on being filled with subsidies for as long as the prospect of an imminent breakthrough can be dangled in front of politicians and the public. Since most people these days consistently mistake technical feasibility for economic viability, there's no shortage of easy marks for this sort of sales pitch.

There are plenty of subsidy dumpsters in the energy field just now. What makes this all the more unfortunate is that quite a few of them are based on technologies that could be used in less self-defeating ways. Solar power, to name only one example, could make a huge dent in America's energy needs, if the available resources focused on proven technologies such as solar water heaters; once this sensible approach is replaced by attempts to claim that we can keep the grid powered by paving some substantial fraction of Nevada with solar PV cells, though, we're in subsidy-dumpster territory, as a recent study of Spain's much-lauded solar program has shown. Renewable energy is a viable option so long as its sharp limits of concentration and intermittency are kept in mind; ignore those, and pretend that we can keep on living today's extravagant lifestyles on a basis that won't support them, and you've got a perfect recipe for a subsidy dumpster.

Now it's only fair to point out that the energy issue is far from the only dimension of modern life that attracts subsidy dumpsters. Name a current crisis here in America—joblessness, urban blight, decaying infrastructure, and the list goes on—and there are plenty of subsidy dumpsters to be found, some empty and rusting like yesterday's ethanol plants, some soaking up government funds like the ITER project, and many more that are still only a twinkle in the eyes of their eager promoters. Still, I'd like to suggest that subsidy dumpsters in the energy field have a particular importance just now.

The end of the age of cheap abundant energy requires that we stop using anything like as much energy as we've been using in recent decades. Any approach to dealing with the crisis of our age that doesn't start by using much less energy, in other words, simply isn't serious. The parade of subsidy dumpsters being hawked to politicians these days is merely one more attempt to refuse to take our predicament as seriously as it deserves, and thus serves mostly as a way to make that predicament even worse than it has to be. By and large, to borrow a neatly Pharaonic turn of phrase from one of my longtime readers—tip of the archdruidical hat to Robin Datta—that's the trouble with spending all your time splashing around in the waters of denial; all that happens, in the final analysis, is that you attract the attention of the crocodiles of reality.

Refusing the Call:
A Tale Rewritten
(Originally published 23 April 2014)

I have been wondering for some time now how to talk about the weirdly autumnal tone that sounds so often and so clearly in America these days. Through the babble and clatter, the seven or eight television screens yelling from the walls of every restaurant you pass and all the rest of it, there comes a mood by turns shrill, sullen, and self-pitying, as though even the people who insist most loudly that it's all onward and upward from here don't believe it any more, and those for whom the old optimism stopped being more than a soothing shibboleth a long time ago are hunching their shoulders, shutting their eyes tight, and hoping that things can still hold together for just a little while longer.

It's not just that American politicians and pundits are insisting at the top of their lungs that the United States can threaten Russia with natural gas surpluses that don't exist, though that's admittedly a very bad sign all by itself. It's that this orgy of self-congratulatory nonsense appears in the news right next to reports that oil and gas companies are slashing their investments in the fracking technology and shale leases that were supposed to produce those imaginary surpluses, having lost a great deal of money pursuing the shale oil mirage, while Russia and Iran pursue trade deals that will make US sanctions against both countries all but irrelevant, and China is quietly arranging to conduct its trade with Europe in yuan rather than dollars. Strong nations in control of their own destinies, it's fair to note, don't respond to challenges on this scale by plunging their heads quite so enthusiastically into the sands of self-deception.

That is to say, the long day of national delusion that dawned back in 1980, when Ronald Reagan famously and fatuously proclaimed "it's morning in America," is drawing on rapidly toward dusk, and most Americans are hopelessly unprepared for the coming of night. They're unprepared in practical terms, that is, for an era in which the five per cent of us who live in the United States will no longer dispose of a quarter of the world's energy supply and a third of its raw materials and industrial products, and in which what currently counts as a normal American lifestyle will soon be no more than a fading memory for the vast majority. They're just as unprepared, though, for the psychological and emotional costs of that shattering transformation—not least because the change isn't being imposed on them at random by an indifferent universe, but comes as the inevitable consequence of their own collective choices in decades not that long past.

The hard fact that most people in this country are trying not to remember is this: in the years right after Reagan's election, a vast number of Americans enthusiastically turned their backs on the promising steps toward sustainability that had been taken in the previous decade, abandoned the ideals they'd been praising to the skies up to that time, and cashed in their grandchildrens' future so that they didn't have to give up the extravagance and waste that defined their familiar and comfortable lifestyles. As a direct result, the nonrenewable resources that might have supported the transition to a sustainable future went instead to fuel one last orgy of wretched excess. Now, though, the party is over, the bill is due, and the consequences of that disastrous decision have become a massive though almost wholly unmentionable factor in our nation's culture and collective psychology.

servants, or what have you.

So he refused, and when Gandalf tried to talk to him about it, he threw the old wizard out of Bag End and slammed the round green door in his face. Have you ever seen someone in a fight who knows that he's in the wrong, and knows that everyone else knows it, and that knowledge just makes him even more angry and stubborn? That was Frodo just then. Friends of mine watched the whole thing, or as much of it as could be seen from the garden outside, and it was not a pleasant spectacle.

It's what happened thereafter, though, that bears recalling. I'm quite sure that if Frodo had shown the least sign of leaving the Shire and going on the quest, Sauron would have sent Black Riders after him in a fine hurry, and there's no telling what else might have come boiling up out of Mordor. It's by no means impossible that the Dark Lord might have panicked, and launched a hasty, ill-advised assault on Gondor right away. For all I know, that may have been what Gandalf had in mind, tricking the Dark Lord into overreacting before he'd gathered his full strength, and before Gondor and Rohan had been thoroughly weakened from within.

Still, once Sauron's spies brought him word that Frodo had refused to embark on the quest, the Dark Lord knew that he had a good deal less to fear, and that he could afford to take his time. Ever since then, there have been plenty of servants of Mordor in and around the Shire, and a Black Rider or two keeping watch nearby, but nothing obvious or direct, nothing that might rouse whatever courage Frodo might have had left or convince him that he had to flee for his life. Sauron was willing to be patient—patient and cruel. I'm quite sure he knew perfectly well what the rest of Frodo's life would be like.

So Gandalf went away, and Frodo stayed in Bag End, and for years thereafter it seemed as though the whole business had been no more than a mistake. The news that came up the Greenway from the southern lands was no worse than before; Gondor still stood firm, and though there was said to be some kind of trouble in Rohan, well, that was only to be expected now and then. Frodo even took to joking about how gullible he'd been to believe all those alarmist claims that Gandalf had made. Sauron was still safely cooped up in Mordor, and all seemed right with Middle-earth.

Of course part of that was simply that Frodo had gotten even wealthier and more comfortable than he'd been before. He patched up his relationship with the Sackville-Bagginses, and he invested a good deal of his money in Sandyman's mill in Hobbiton, which paid off handsomely. He no longer spent time with many of his younger friends by then, partly because they had their own opinions about what he should have done, and partly because he had business connections with some of the wealthiest hobbits in the Shire, and wanted to build on those. He no longer took long walks around the Shire, as he'd done before, and he gave up visiting elves and dwarves when he stopped speaking to Gandalf.

But of course the rumors and news from the southern lands slowly but surely turned to the worse, as the Dark Lord gathered his power and tightened his grip on the western lands a little at a time. I recall when Rohan fell to Saruman's goblin armies. That was a shock for a great many folk, here in the Shire and elsewhere. Soon thereafter, though, Frodo was claiming that after all, Saruman wasn't Sauron, and Rohan wasn't that important, and for all anyone knew, the wizard and the Dark Lord might well end up at each other's throats and spare the rest of us.

Still, it was around that time that Frodo stopped joking about Gandalf's warnings, and got angry if anyone mentioned them in his hearing. It was around that same time, too, that he started insisting loudly and often that someone would surely stop Sauron. One day it was the elves: after all, they had three rings of power, and could surely overwhelm the forces of Mordor if they chose to. Another day, the dwarves would do it, or Saruman, or the men of Gondor, or the Valar in the uttermost West. There were so many alternatives!

His friends very quickly learned to nod and agree with him, for he would lose his temper and start shouting at them if they disagreed or even asked questions.

When Lorien was destroyed, that was another shock. It was after that, as I recall, that Frodo started hinting darkly that the elves didn't seem to be doing anything with their three rings of power to stop Sauron, and maybe they weren't as opposed to him as they claimed. He came up with any number of theories about this or that elvish conspiracy. The first troubles were starting to affect the Shire by then, of course, and his investments were beginning to lose money; it was probably inevitable that he would start claiming that the conspiracy was aimed in part against hobbits, against the Shire, or against him in particular—especially the latter. They wanted his Ring, of course. That played a larger and larger role in his talk as the years passed.

I don't recall hearing of any particular change in his thinking when word came that Minas Tirith had been taken by the Dark Lord's armies, but it wasn't much later that a great many elves came hurrying along the East Road through the Shire, and a few months after that, word came that Rivendell had fallen. That was not merely a shock, but a blow; Frodo had grown up hearing his uncle's stories about Rivendell and the elves and half-elves who lived there. There was a time after that news came that some of us briefly wondered if old Frodo might actually find it in himself to do the thing he'd refused to do all those years before.

But of course he did nothing of the kind, not even when the troubles here in the Shire began to bite more and more deeply, when goblins started raiding the borders of the North Farthing and the Buckland had to be abandoned to the Old Forest. No, he started insisting to anyone who would listen that Middle-earth was doomed, that there was no hope left in elves or dying Númenor, that Sauron's final victory would surely come before—oh, I forget what the date was; it was some year or other not too far from now. He spent hours reading through books of lore, making long lists of reasons why the Dark Lord's triumph was surely at hand. Why did he do that? Why, for the same reason that drove him to each of his other excuses in turn: to prove to himself that his decision to refuse the quest hadn't been the terrible mistake he knew perfectly well it had been.

And then, of course, the Ring betrayed him, as it betrayed Gollum and Isildur before him. He came home late at night, after drinking himself half under the table at the Ivy Bush, and discovered that the Ring was nowhere to be found. After searching Bag End in a frantic state, he ran out the door and down the road toward Bywater shouting "My precious! My precious!" He was weeping and running blindly in the night, and when he got to the bridge he stumbled; over he went into the water, and that was the end of him. They found his body in a weir downstream the next morning.

The worst of it is that right up to the end, right up to the hour the Ring left him, he still could have embarked on the quest. It would have been a different journey, and quite possibly a harder one. With Rivendell gone, he would have had to go west rather than east, across the Far Downs to Cirdan at the Grey Havens, where you'll find most of the high-elves who still remain in Middle-earth. From there, with such companions as might have joined him, he would have had to go north and then eastward through Arnor, past the ruins of Annuminas and Lake Evendim, to the dales of the Misty Mountains, and then across by one of the northern passes: a hard and risky journey, but by no means impossible, for with no more need to hinder travel between Rivendell and Lorien, the Dark Lord's watch on the mountains has grown slack.

Beyond the mountains, the wood-elves still dwell in the northern reaches of Mirkwood, along with refugees from Lorien and the last of the Beornings. He could have gotten shelter and help there, and boats to travel down the River Running into the heart of Wilderland. From there his way would have led by foot to the poorly guarded northern borders of Mordor—when has Sauron ever had to face a threat from that quarter? So you see that it could have been done. It could still be done, if someone were willing to do it. Even though so much of what could have been saved thirty years ago has been lost, even though Minas Tirith, Edoras, Lorien and Rivendell have fallen and the line of the kings of Gondor is no more, it would still be worth doing; there would still be many things that could be saved.

Nor would such a journey have to be made alone. Though Aragorn son of Arathorn was slain in the last defense of Rivendell, there are still Rangers to be found in Cirdan's realm and the old lands of Arnor; there are elf-warriors who hope to avenge the blood shed at Rivendell, and dwarves from the Blue Mountains who have their own ancient grudges against the Dark Lord. The last free Rohirrim retreated to Minhiriath after Éomer fell at Helm's Deep, and still war against King Grima, while Gondor west of the river Gilrain clings to a tenuous independence and would rise up against Sauron at need. Would those and the elves of Lindon be enough? No one can say; there are no certainties in this business, except for the one Frodo chose—the certainty that doing nothing will guarantee Sauron's victory.

And there might even still be a wizard to join such a quest. In fact, there would certainly be one—the very last of them, as far as I know. Gandalf perished when Lorien fell, I am sorry to say, and as for Saruman, the last anyone saw of him, he was screaming in terror as two Ringwraiths dragged him through the door of the Dark Tower; his double-dealing was never likely to bring him to a good end. The chief of the Ringwraiths rules in Isengard now. Still, there was a third in these western lands: fool and bird-tamer, Saruman called him, having never quite managed to notice that knowledge of the ways of nature and the friendship of birds and beasts might have considerable value in the last need of Middle-earth. Radagast is his name; yes, that would be me.

Why am I telling you all this? Well, you are old Frodo's youngest cousin, are you not? Very nearly the only one of his relatives with enough of the wild Tookish blood in you to matter, or so I am told. It was just a month ago that you and two of your friends were walking in the woods, and you spoke with quite a bit of anger about how the older generation of hobbits had decided to huddle in their holes until the darkness falls—those were your very words, I believe. How do I know that? Why, a little bird told me—a wren, to be precise, a very clever and helpful little fellow, who runs errands for me from time to time when I visit this part of Middle-earth. If you meant what you said then, there is still hope.

And the Ring? No, it was not lost, or not for long. It slipped from its chain and fell from old Frodo's pocket as he stumbled home that last night, and a field mouse spotted it. I had briefed all the animals and birds around Hobbiton, of course, and so she knew what to do; she dragged the Ring into thick grass, and when dawn came, caught the attention of a jay, who took it and hid it high up in a tree. I had to trade quite a collection of sparkling things for it! But here it is, in this envelope, waiting for someone to take up the quest that Frodo refused. The choice is yours, my dear hobbit. What will you do?

The Time of the Seedbearers

(Originally published 30 April 2014)

Myths, according to the philosopher Sallust, are things that never happened but always are. With a few modifications, the same rule applies to the enduring narratives of every culture, the stories that find a new audience in every generation as long as their parent cultures last. Stories of that stature don't need to chronicle events that actually took place to have something profoundly relevant to say, and the heroic quest I used last week to frame a satire on the embarrassingly unheroic behavior of many of industrial civilization's more privileged inmates is no exception to that rule.

That's true of hero tales generally, of course. The thegns and ceorls who sat spellbound in an Anglo-Saxon meadhall while a scop chanted the deeds of Beowulf to the sound of a six-stringed lyre didn't have to face the prospect of wrestling with cannibalistic ogres or battling fire-breathing dragons, and were doubtless well aware of that fact. If they believed that terrible creatures of a kind no longer found once existed in the legendary past, why, so do we—the difference in our case is merely that we call our monsters "dinosaurs," and insist that our paleontologist-storytellers be prepared to show us the bones.

The audience in the meadhall never wondered whether Beowulf was a historical figure in the same sense as their own great-

221

grandparents. Since history and legend hadn't yet separated out in the thinking of the time, Beowulf and those great-grandparents occupied exactly the same status, that of people in the past about whom stories were told. Further than that it was unnecessary to go, since what mattered to them about Beowulf was not whether he lived but how he lived. The tale's original audience, it's worth recalling, got up the next morning to face the challenges of life in dark age Britain, in which defending their communities against savage violence was a commonplace event; having the example of Beowulf's courage and loyalty in mind must have made that harsh reality a little easier to face.

The same point can be made about the hero tale I borrowed and rewrote in last week's post, Tolkien's *The Lord of the Rings*. Frodo Baggins was no Beowulf, which was of course exactly the point, since Tolkien was writing for a different audience in a different age. The experience of being wrenched out of a peaceful community and sent on a long march toward horror and death was one that Tolkien faced as a young man in the First World War, and watched his sons face in the Second. That's what gave Tolkien's tale its appeal: his hobbits were ordinary people facing extraordinary challenges, like so many people in the bitter years of the early twentieth century.

The contrast between *Beowulf* and *The Lord of the Rings* is precisely that between the beginning and the zenith of a civilization. Beowulf, like his audience, was born into an age of chaos and violence, and there was never any question of what he was supposed to do about it; the only detail that had to be settled was how many of the horrors of his time he would overcome before one of them finally killed him. Frodo Baggins, like his audience, was born into a world that was mostly at peace, but found itself faced with a resurgence of a nightmare that everyone in his community thought had been laid to rest for good. In Frodo's case, the question of what he was going to do about the crisis of his age was what mattered most—and of course that's why I was able to stand Tolkien's narrative on its head last week, by tracing out what would have happened if Frodo's answer had been different.

Give it a few more centuries, and it's a safe bet that the stories that matter will be back on Beowulf's side of the equation, as the process of decline and fall now under way leads into an era of dissolution and rebirth that we might as well call by the time-honored label "dark age." For the time being, though, most of us are still on Frodo's side of things, trying to come to terms with the appalling realization that the world we know is coming apart and it's up to us to do something about it.

That said, there's a crucial difference between the situation faced by Frodo Baggins and his friends in Middle-earth, and the situation faced by those of us who have awakened to the crisis of our time here and now. Tolkien was a profoundly conservative thinker and writer, in the full sense of that word. The plot engine of his works of adult fiction, *The Silmarillion* just as much as *The Lord of the Rings*, was always the struggle to hold onto the last scraps of a glorious past, and his powers of evil want to make Middle-earth modern, efficient and up-to-date by annihilating the past and replacing it with a cutting-edge industrial landscape of slagheaps and smokestacks. It's thus no accident that Saruman's speech to Gandalf in book two, chapter two of *The Fellowship of the Ring* is a parody of the modern rhetoric of progress, or that *The Return of the King* ends with a Luddite revolt against Sharkey's attempted industrialization of the Shire; Tolkien was a keen and acerbic observer of twentieth-century England, and wove much of his own political thought into his stories.

The victory won by Tolkien's protagonists in *The Lord of the Rings*, accordingly, amounted to restoring Middle-Earth as far as possible to the condition it was in before the War of the Ring, with the clock turned back a bit further here and there—for example, the reestablishment of the monarchy in Gondor—and a keen sense of loss surrounding those changes that couldn't be undone. That was a reasonable goal in Tolkien's imagined setting, and it's understandable that so many people want to achieve the same thing here and now: to preserve some semblance of industrial civilization in the teeth of the rising spiral of crises that are already beginning to tear it apart.

I can sympathize with their desire. It's become fashionable in many circles to ignore the achievements of the industrial age and focus purely on its failures, or to fixate on the places where it fell short of the frankly Utopian hopes that clustered around its rise. If the Enlightenment turned out to be far more of a mixed blessing than its more enthusiastic prophets liked to imagine, and if so many achievements of science and technology turned into sources of immense misery once they were whored out in the service of greed and political power, the same can be said of most human things: "If it has passed from the high and the beautiful to darkness and ruin," Tolkien commented of a not dissimilar trajectory, "that was of old the fate of Arda marred."[*] Still, the window of opportunity through which modern industrial civilization might have been able to escape its unwelcome destiny has long since slammed shut.

That's one of the things I meant to suggest in last week's post by sketching out a Middle-earth already ravaged by the Dark Lord, in which most of the heroes of Tolkien's trilogy were dead and most of the things they fought to save had already been lost. Even with those changes, though, Tolkien's narrative no longer fits the crisis of our age as well as it did a few decades back. Our Ring of Power was the fantastic glut of energy we got from fossil fuels; we could have renounced it, as Tolkien's characters renounced the One Ring, before we'd burnt enough to destabilize the climate and locked ourselves into a set of economic arrangements with no future...but that's not what happened, of course.

We didn't make that collective choice when it still could have made a difference: when peak oil was still decades in the future,

---

[*] J.R.R. Tolkien, *The Silmarillion* (New York: Ballantine Books, 1977), p.316.

anthropogenic climate change hadn't yet begun to destabilize the planet's ice sheets and weather patterns, and the variables that define the crisis of our age—depletion rates, CO_2 concentrations, global population, and the rest of them—were a good deal less overwhelming than they've now become. As *The Limits to Growth* pointed out more than four decades ago, any effort to extract industrial civilization from the trap it made for itself had to get under way long before the jaws of that trap began to bite, because the rising economic burden inflicted by the ongoing depletion of nonrenewable resources and the impacts of pollution and ecosystem degradation were eating away at the surplus wealth needed to meet the costs of the transition to sustainability.

That prediction has now become our reality. Grandiose visions of vast renewable-energy buildouts and geoengineering projects on a global scale, of the kind being hawked so ebulliently these days by the prophets of eternal business as usual, fit awkwardly with the reality that a great many industrial nations can no longer afford to maintain basic infrastructures or to keep large and growing fractions of their populations from sliding into desperate poverty. The choice that I discussed in last week's post, reduced to its hard economic bones, was whether we were going to put what remained of our stock of fossil fuels and other nonrenewable resources into maintaining our current standard of living for a while longer, or whether we were going to put it into building a livable world for our grandchildren.

The great majority of us chose the first option, and insisting at the top of our lungs that of course we could have both did nothing to keep the second from slipping away into the realm of might-have-beens. The political will to make the changes and accept the sacrifices that would be required to do anything else went missing in action in the 1980s and hasn't been seen since. That's the trap that was hidden in the crisis of our age: while the costs of transition were still small enough that we could have met them without major sacrifice, the consequences of inaction were still far enough in the future that most people could pretend they weren't there; by the time the consequences were hard to ignore, the costs of transition had become too great for most people to accept—and not too long after that, they had become too great to be met at all. .

As a commentary on our current situation, in other words, the story of the heroic quest has passed its pull date. As I noted years ago, insisting that the world must always follow a single narrative is a fertile source of misunderstanding and misery. Consider the popular insistence that the world can grow its way out of problems caused by growth—as though you could treat the consequences of chronic alcoholism by drinking even more heavily! What gives that frankly idiotic claim the appeal it has is that it draws on one of the standard stories of our age, the Horatio Alger story of the person who overcame long odds to make a success of himself. That does happen sometimes, which is why it's a popular story; the lie creeps in when the claim gets made that this is *always* what happens.

When people insist, as so many of them do, that of course we'll overcome the limits to growth and every other obstacle to our allegedly preordained destiny out there among the stars, all that means is that they have a single story wedged into their imagination so tightly that mere reality can't shake it loose. The same thing's true of all the other credos I've discussed in recent posts, from "they'll think of something" through "it's all somebody else's fault" right on up to "we're all going to be extinct soon anyway so it doesn't matter any more." Choose any thoughtstopper you like, and behind it lies a single story, repeating itself monotonously over and over in the heads of those who can't imagine the world unfolding in any other way.

The insistence that it's not too late, that there must still be time to keep industrial civilization from crashing into ruin if only we all come together to make one great effort, and that there's any reason to think that we can and will all come together, is another example. The

226

narrative behind that claim has a profound appeal to people nowadays, which is why stories that feature it—again, Tolkien's trilogy comes to mind—are as popular as they are. It's deeply consoling to be told that there's still one last chance to escape the harsh future that's already taking shape around us. It seems almost cruel to point out that whether a belief appeals to our emotions has no bearing on whether or not it's true.

The suggestion that I've been making since this blog first began eight years ago is that we're long past the point at which modern industrial civilization might still have been rescued from the consequences of its own mistakes. If that's the case, it's no longer useful to put the very limited resources we have left into trying to stop the inevitable, and it's even less useful to wallow in wishful thinking about how splendid it would be if the few of us who recognize the predicament we're in were to be joined by enough other people to make a difference. If anything of value is to get through the harsh decades and centuries ahead of us, if anything worth saving is to be rescued from the wreck of our civilization, there's plenty of work to do, and daydreaming about mass movements that aren't happening and grand projects we can no longer afford simply wastes what little time we still have left.

That's why I've tried to suggest in previous posts here that it's time to set aside some of our more familiar stories and try reframing the crisis of our age in less shopworn ways. There are plenty of viable options—plenty, that is, of narratives that talk about what happens when the last hope of rescue has gone whistling down the wind and it's time to figure out what can be saved in the midst of disaster—but the one that keeps coming back to my mind is one I learned and, ironically, dismissed as uninteresting quite a few decades ago, in the early years of my esoteric studies: the old legend of the fall of Atlantis.

It's probably necessary to note here that whether Atlantis existed as a historical reality is not the point. While it's interesting to speculate about whether human societies more advanced than current theory suggests might have flourished in the late Ice Age and then drowned beneath rising seas, those speculations are as irrelevant here as trying to fit Grendel and his mother into the family tree of the Hominidae, say, or discussing how plate tectonics could have produced the improbable mountain ranges of Middle-earth. Whatever else it might or might not have been, Atlantis is a story, one that has a potent presence in our collective imagination. Like *Beowulf* or *The Lord of the Rings*, the Atlantis story is about the confrontation with evil, but where Beowulf comes at the beginning of a civilization and Frodo Baggins marks its zenith, the Atlantis story illuminates its end.

Mind you, the version of the story of Atlantis I learned, in common with most of the versions in circulation in occult schools in those days, had three details that you won't find in Plato's account, or in most of the rehashes that have been churned out by the rejected-knowledge industry over the last century or so. First, according to that version, Atlantis didn't sink all at once; rather, there were three inundations separated by long intervals. Second, the sinking of Atlantis wasn't a natural disaster; it was the direct result of the clueless actions of the Atlanteans, who brought destruction on themselves by their misuse of advanced technology.

The third detail, though, is the one that matters here. According to the mimeographed lessons I studied back in the day, as it became clear that Atlantean technology had the potential to bring about terrifying blowback, the Atlanteans divided into two factions: the Children of the Law of One, who took the warnings seriously and tried to get the rest of Atlantean society to do so, and the Servants of the Dark Face, who dismissed the whole issue—I don't know for a fact that these latter went around saying "I'm sure the priests of the Sun Temple will think of something," "orichalcum will always be with us," "the ice age wasn't ended by an ice shortage," and the like, but it seems likely. Those of my readers who haven't spent the last forty years hiding at the bottom of the sea will know instantly which of these factions spoke for the majority and which was marginalized and derided as a bunch of doomers.

According to the story, when the First Inundation hit and a big chunk of Atlantis ended up permanently beneath the sea, the shock managed to convince a lot of Atlanteans that the Children of the Law of One had a point, and for a while there was an organized effort to stop doing the things that were causing the blowback. As the immediate memories of the Inundation faded, though, people convinced themselves that the flooding had just been one of those things, and went back to their old habits. When the Second Inundation followed and all of Atlantis sank but the two big islands of Ruta and Daitya, though, the same pattern didn't repeat itself; the Children of the Law of One were marginalized even further, and the Servants of the Dark Face became even more of a majority, because nobody wanted to admit the role their own actions had had in causing the catastrophe. Again, those of my readers who have been paying attention for the last forty years know this story inside and out.

It's what happened next, though, that matters most. In the years between the Second Inundation and the Third and last one, so the story goes, Atlantis was for all practical purposes a madhouse with the inmates in charge. Everybody knew what was going to happen and nobody wanted to deal with the implications of that knowledge, and the strain expressed itself in orgiastic excess, bizarre belief systems, and a rising spiral of political conflict ending in civil war—anything you care to name, as long as it didn't address the fact that Atlantis was destroying itself and that nearly all the Atlanteans were enthusiastic participants in the activities driving the destruction. That was when the Children of the Law of One looked at one another and, so to speak, cashed out their accounts at the First National Bank of Atlantis, invested the proceeds in shipping, and sailed off to distant lands to become the seedbearers of the new age of the world.

That's the story that speaks to me just now—enough so that I've more than once considered writing a fantasy novel about the fall of Atlantis as a way of talking about the crisis of our age. Of course that story doesn't speak to everyone, and the belief systems that insist either that everything is fine or that nothing can be done anyway have no shortage of enthusiasts. If these belief systems turn out to be as delusional as they look, though, what then? The future that very few people are willing to consider or prepare for is the one that history shows us is the common destiny of every other failed civilization: the long, bitter, ragged road of decline and fall into a dark age, from which future civilizations will eventually be born. If that's the future ahead of us, as I believe it is, the necessary preparations need to be made now, if the best achievements of our age are to be carried into the future when the time of the seedbearers arrives.

An *Archdruid Report* Bibliography

The following books all derive core themes, and in some cases a fair amount of rough-draft prose, from sequences of weekly *Archdruid Report* posts. All are written by me except the *After Oil* series, which are anthologies of SF short stories written by readers of *The Archdruid Report*; *Star's Reach* and *Twilight's Last Gleaming* are novels, and the rest are nonfiction.

The Long Descent: A User's Guide to the End of the Industrial Age (New Society, 2008)

The Ecotechnic Future: Envisioning a Post-Peak World (New Society, 2009)

The Wealth of Nature: Economics As If Survival Mattered (New Society, 2011)

The Blood of the Earth: An Essay on Magic and Peak Oil (Scarlet Imprint, 2012)

Not The Future We Ordered: Peak Oil, Psychology, and the Myth of Progress (Karnac Publications, 2013)

After Oil: SF Visions of the Post-Petroleum World (Founders House, 2012)

231

Green Wizardry (New Society, 2013)

Star's Reach: A Novel of the Deindustrial Future (Founders House, 2014)

Decline and Fall: The End of Empire and the Future of Democracy in 21st Century America (New Society, 2014).

Twilight's Last Gleaming (Karnac Publications, 2014)

After Progress: Reason and Religion at the End of the Industrial Age (New Society, 2015)

After Oil 2: The Years of Crisis (Founders House, 2015)

After Oil 3: The Years of Renewal (Founders House, 2015)

Index

About The Author

John Michael Greer is the author of more than thirty books, including four books on peak oil and two science fiction novels, *The Fires of Shalsha* and *Star's Reach*, as well as the weekly peak oil blog *The Archdruid Report*. A native of the Pacific Northwest, he now lives in an old red brick mill town in the north central Appalachians with his wife Sara.

Printed in Great Britain
by Amazon

66112121R00147